THICK AS THIEVES

HILARIOUS TALES OF RIDICULOUS ROBBERS, BUNGLING BURGLARS AND INCOMPETENT CONMEN

D1078564

ANDREW PENMAN

MONDAY BOOKS

A CIP catalogue record for this title is available from the British Library

ISBN: 978-1-906308-58-2

Typeset by Andrew Searle

Printed and bound by CPI Group (UK) Ltd

www.mondaybooks.com
http://mondaybooks.wordpress.com/
info@mondaybooks.com

INTRODUCTION

I'VE HAD A FAIR amount of experience of crooks – some fairly minor, some more serious.

For instance, a couple of years back I was returning home from a night out in London with my wife. As we left the tube station through two ticket barriers next to each other, I felt someone push behind me. It was a bloke, tail-gating me through the barrier, and his girlfriend had done the same thing to my wife at the same moment. He turned and laughed as they left the station. It's not the biggest crime in the world, though every fare-dodger raises the prices for the rest of us, but for some reason it sticks in my mind; it's up there, illogically, with the three times my car was vandalised, the time I was burgled (on New Year's Eve, a great start to the year), and the night I was mugged and ended up going to hospital in an ambulance.

I don't claim any special victim status here; that's probably about average for someone who lived in south London for 20 years. But it has given me a small personal motivation in the writing of this book, along with that handed me by the victimised people whose stories I tell in my column in *The Daily Mirror*. We try to expose conmen, fraudsters and charlatans who rip off our readers, and I know the grief that these parasites cause, particularly to the poor, elderly and vulnerable. Sometimes they'll fleece their victims of their life savings – other times it might only be ten or twenty quid. Whatever the amount, the victims are left with the sickening, shattering knowledge that someone has carefully set out to rob or con them, and succeeded. 'I feel so stupid,' victims of crime frequently tell me.

I recall confronting one conman for a story for the *Mirror* and asking him how he felt about his bewildered victims, who were often reduced to tears of fear and anger.

His reply was, 'I don't give a toss.'

One of his accomplices said, 'What's not nice? That we are ripping off stupid people? If they're f***ing stupid they deserve it.'

Crooks love this argument, that victims of crime are somehow the authors of their own misfortune. Of course, it's obscene; they're really taking advantage of the common trust that greases the wheels of everyday interaction.

But let's take them at their word – and then turn the argument on its head by putting the stupidity of criminals under the spotlight.

Some might feel my tone is malicious, or vindictive. Perhaps it is – but, if so, here's one of many reasons I might feel that way. This letter, combining callousness and stupidity, was written by a 16-year-old burglar to his victim:

> Dear Victim,
> I dont no Why Iam Writing a letter to you! I have been forced to Write this letter by ISSP [Intensive Supervision and Surveillance Programme]. To be honest I'm not bothered or sorry about the fact that I burlged your houSe. Basicly it was your fault anyways. I'm going to run you through the dumb mistakes you made.
> Firstly you didnt draw your curtains which most people now to do before they go to sleep.
> Secondly your dumb you live in Stainburns a high risk burglary area and you thick enough to leave your downstairs kitchen window open. I wouldnt do that in a million years.
> But anyways I dont feel Sorry for you and Im not going to show any sympath or remores.
> Yours sincerely.

Could any degree of public humiliation be too much for the author of that infantile and heartless letter? Unfortunately, at 16 he must remain anonymous – but something tells me that before very long he'll be up in an adult court where he can be named. I hope the judge doesn't show him any *sympath*.

Some readers might feel that I am being unfair to the poor thickies who grace the following pages. As a pinko liberal, I struggle with this myself. Should we not try to understand them? Isn't some serious analysis needed? After all, an official report into the 2011 riots in Britain showed that 48% of the young people arrested left primary school unable to read or write properly, and four out of ten of the rioters in London were unemployed.

But while these *are* disgraceful statistics, how do we explain the fact that the vast majority of people who leave school without decent qualifications do not go on to become burglars, robbers and muggers? And, strictly for the purposes of this book, do we care? Someone should thoroughly examine these important issues, but this is not that book.

My job is not to ponder why, for instance, a young woman decided to exploit the riots by stealing a pair of Nikes – but to share with you the fact that she ran off with two left-footed trainers. It could be that there are wider sociological issues at work here which explain her actions; or maybe it's simply that she was both greedy and stupid. What I can assure you is this: that's the last time you'll come across the word 'sociological' here.

The ways that stupid criminals get themselves caught are too many and varied to summarise in this short introduction, but hopefully you'll find more than enough examples in the pages that follow to satisfy the most vengeful appetite. It's time to put the boot on the other foot, time to shine the spotlight on stupid criminals and bring a little joy into our lives by having a laugh at their expense.

IT'S FAIR TO say that most criminals are pretty lazy.

But they tend to have a bit more gumption than hapless Christopher Walker.

He carried out a pretty decent robbery, actually – stealing £25,000 from a security guard after hitting him with a stick as he delivered cash to a branch of Lloyd's Bank in Birmingham.

Lots of people saw it happen, and then watched in understandable astonishment as Walker ran off straight back to his own house – *which was literally across the road.*

He was arrested a few minutes later by police who knocked on his door. 'It was one of the easier cases I've been involved in,' one detective said.

Walker, 19, from Birmingham, was jailed for two-and-a-half years in November 2009 after admitting robbery.

*

FRANCIS ~~GORMLESS~~ GORMLEY, came up with a cracker of a plan – he wrote to Asda and threatened to poison stock in one of their stores unless they paid him off with £25,000.

His letter said:

> 'I regret to inform you that we have chosen your store, but chosen it we have. The scenario is simple. A number of food items have been purchased from your store. These food items contaninated (sic) with a range of poisonous chemicals are to be placed by us back in your store the results you can imagine. What we want is £25,000, a reasonable sum when weighed against the loss of business and inevitable compensation claims.'

The supermarket giant would surely fold, he reasoned, and he was right.

Asda dropped off the money when and where Gormley, 40, had ordered.

Obviously, they also mentioned it to the police, who lay in wait for the blackmailer to show up to collect his loot.

And it didn't take him long, which isn't a surprise – the designated place for the drop was a planter *in his own front garden*.

The cops – who had been geared up for a high-speed chase – were astonished.

'The idea that he would actually have the ransom money delivered to his own house was something we hadn't bargained for,' admitted a Greater Manchester Police source. 'It really was the height of stupidity, and laziness.'

Gormley, a mature student with gambling debts, was jailed for three years.

*

AN IMPORTANT PART of being a successful robber is choosing the right time and victim.

Jerome Blanchett chose to hold up a policeman at a Holiday Inn which was hosting a narcotics conference involving 300 other policemen – even though there was a big sign outside welcoming all the cops, and the car park was full of their cars.

This was not the right time or victim.

The 19-year-old dumbass followed the NYPD's John Comparetto into the toilets, produced a .40 cal semi-automatic handgun and told him to hand over his cash and valuables. Mr Comparetto did as he was told, and Blanchett then told him to drop his trousers – to hamper any attempt at a chase – and threatened to kill him if he tried.

But as soon as Blanchett had gone, Mr Comparetto pulled up his strides, took his own pistol from its hidden ankle holster, and went after him, with a load of other cops in hot pursuit.

They grabbed him as he was trying to get into a taxi to make good his escape, near the hotel in Swatara, Pennsylvania.

Blanchett was later sentenced to 52 to 104 years in state prison for a series of violent robberies of pizza deliverymen, and a further 30 on top for this escapade.

Mr Comparetto generously described him as 'the stupidest criminal in the state of Pennsylvania.'

*

THE ROBBERS WHO attempted to raid the post office in the *Midsomer Murders* village of Stanton St John, Oxfordshire, definitely got their timing out.

The two men – who have not yet been caught – were wearing hooded tops and wielding a gun and a machete when they confronted shopkeeper Dennis Ingrey and ordered him to open up the sub-post office and hand over all the cash in the safe.

A bemused Mr Ingrey said, 'I told them we didn't have a flipping post office, or a safe. They were six months too late. It was really bizarre. At the time I thought they were idiots.'

Had they timed the raid a bit better they could have made away with about £6,000, he added.

*

NEIL MURRAY GOT the basics right as a getaway driver.

Nick a fast car for the purpose? Check.

Hang around outside the jewellers? Check.

Keep the engine running? Check.

It all went absolutely to plan, until the moment that his mates ran back out of Simon Pure Jewellery Design in Guildford, Surrey, with £60,000-worth of gems – after terrorising a female shop assistant – and leapt into the stolen Alfa Romeo yelling, 'Go! Go! Go!'

Because that was the point when Murray, 34, decided – for reasons only he could explain – to become the world's most law-abiding driver.

Mirror, signal, manoeuvre… and off we go.

Keeping strictly to the speed limit – which was 30mph for much of the way – or even dipping under it, Murray gave the increasingly anxious gang of desperados zero chance of eluding the cops, who had been called by passers-by who had noted down the Alfa's number.

They were all duly arrested within half an hour.

In mitigation at Guildford Crown Court, John Warrington, defending Murray, said, 'The ordeal for the woman lasted less than a minute, and – far from a fast getaway – the police noted that, at times, the car was going under the speed limit.'

The gang got a total of 20 years, with Murray picking up five of them (though he kept his licence clean).

*

AT LEAST MURRAY reached 30mph – that was 10 times quicker than our next gang managed.

Four thieves who broke into 16 boats at a boatyard in St Ives in the early hours of July 2009. They caused £2,500 of damage, pinched a variety of expensive electrical items, including flat screen TVs and generators, plus a lot of booze and a captain's hat, and loaded them onto their getaway… er… punt.

Huntingdon Magistrates' Court heard how they almost topped 3mph as they made good their escape.

They thought they were home and dry, but were nabbed by police officers who used night-vision goggles to watch them floating serenely down the River Ouse.

James Parkinson, 26, and Khushmet Bardell, 24, were jailed, while their teenaged accomplices were ordered to do community work and pay compensation to the owners. Parkinson and Bardell asked for 16 similar offences committed at the boatyard to be taken into consideration.

*

DRUG MULE KAYTI Dryer came up with an innovative place to hide a kilo of cocaine worth £83,000 when she flew into Manchester Airport from the Caribbean.

She – or whoever she was working for – had cut open the hollow shafts of a set of golf clubs, packed the coke inside, and then rewelded them together.

10

And she might have got away with it, but for one small problem.

As the clubs were taken from her to be x-rayed, the customs officer asked the obvious question: 'So... what's your handicap?'

Any golfer would instantly understand, and any intelligent criminal would have taken the trouble to learn a bit of golf lingo.

But Dryer was stumped. 'Er... what do you mean?' she replied.

Clearly, she wasn't a golfer... So why did she have a set of clubs with her?

The officer soon found the welds, and then the drugs, and Dryer was on her way to court and a four year spell in prison.

An airport source told the *Daily Mail* that she claimed she'd taken the clubs on holiday to Montego Bay in Jamaica. 'When asked about her handicap, she looked blank and asked them to repeat the question. She had no idea it was even a golfing term. She thought they were asking her if she had a disability.'

*

CONVICTED CONMAN PETER Clarke and his girlfriend, Sharon Arthurs-Chegini, suffered an extreme case of poetic justice when they pinched a luxury yacht from Villa Nore in Portugal and sailed off into the Atlantic.

They were on bail for a series of frauds – Clarke had already been to prison twice – and the theft of another yacht in Cornwall when they fled to the continent and stole the second boat, the *Skipper VII*.

Unfortunately, they forgot one thing – neither of them knew much about sailing.

No-one heard from them until several months later, when their badly decomposed bodies were found aboard the yacht, which was drifting off the coast of Senegal in western Africa.

It was thought that they might have been killed by pirates, but a 2009 inquest in Truro heard that the pair had probably died from dehydration.

Arthurs-Chegini kept a diary which said they had resorted to drinking their own urine, and had not eaten for four weeks.

'The lights are going out in my heart,' she wrote. 'I dream of my mum's steak-and-kidney pie, roast dinner and sausage and mash.'

*

DERRICK KOSCH strode into the Village Pantry convenience food store in Kokomo, Indiana, at 4.30am one January day in 2008 with evil in his heart, and a gun in his hand.

Brandishing the semi-automatic pistol and putting on his best bad-boy face, the 25-year-old demanded cash and cigarettes from the terrified shop assistant – who meekly did as she was told, and handed over the loot.

'Damned straight!' snarled Kosch, jamming the pistol into the waistband of his trousers.

That's when things went slightly awry.

As he inserted the gun, he inadvertently pulled the trigger, and shot off his own right testicle. (The CCTV footage is still available online, and makes amusing watching.)

Yelping and hopping about in pain, with the round still embedded in his thigh and blood gushing everywhere, he limped to his granny's house, leaving a handy trail for the highly-trained local police to follow.

When he got there, he told her that someone had been trying to rob *him*, but she was a wise old bird and didn't believe a word of it. Her scepticism was rewarded a few moments later, when officers arrived and arrested Kosch, taking him to jail (via hospital, where he underwent emergency surgery).

He later claimed that he carried out the robbery after losing his job and car, and because he felt ashamed at leeching off the woman he lived with.

He served three years for the offence, and on his release told reporters, 'It was shameful and embarrassing, and I think anyone with a good heart would feel that way about it.'

*

OBVIOUSLY, THAT WAS an isolated incident.

Not.

The exotically-named Trinidad Ramos shot at a woman in the doorway of her apartment in Salem, Oregon in June 2010, with one of the rounds hitting her in the leg.

Then he ran back to his white Lincoln Towncar, climbed inside and shot himself in the groin – in much the same way as Mr Kosch.

He was rushed to hospital, and arrested on his release on suspicion of attempted murder, being a felon in possession of a firearm and attempted assault.

In December of that year, he was jailed for 15 years.

*

THEN THERE WAS David Leroy Blurton.

He also shot himself in the groin – this time in the street in Dillon, Colorado.

No-one – including him, he was smashed out of his face at the time – knows exactly why he took the Makarov 9mm pistol from his truck on the evening of May 29, 2009. He'd been on the razz with a chum to celebrate being paid a large sum of money for a job he'd finished. Next thing he knew, he was waking up in the street with a stranger peering over him saying, 'That looks nasty!'

Blurton later claimed he had been the victim of a mugging, but this was not borne out by CCTV images, and there were no witnesses.

He pleaded guilty to the felony charge of reckless discharge of a firearm and the lesser offence of being drunk with a gun.

He was looking at up to three years in prison, but the prosecution settled for probation and the removal of all weapons from his house.

*

RAPE IS NEVER funny – with the possible exception of when the rapist accidentally shoots himself during the act.

Sadly, Washington pervert Jon Newman didn't hit himself in the same place as the aforementioned trio, but still…

Newman snuck up on his victim as she made a mobile phone call outside her house late one night in June, 2009.

Whipping out a pistol, he held it to her head and forced her inside.

In the ensuing struggle, he shot himself.

Unfortunately, the bullet only went into his arm – but it was enough to make him forget all about his rape idea and leg it, howling.

He was later caught, convicted on rape, robbery and gun charges, and jailed for 12 years.

*

JOHN GIBBS WENT one better than all of the above – or, from his point of view, one worse – when he staged a heist at the upmarket Clarke Cooke House restaurant in Newport, Rhode Island, in August 1975.

The 22-year-old ne'er-do-well pulled a nylon stocking over his head, and burst into the office above the famous waterside eaterie and pointed a revolver at manager Jan Buchner.

'Open the safe!' he yelled.

Mr Buchner did as he was told and handed over a roll of quarters and some banknotes, but as Gibbs was stuffing them into his breast pocket he somehow pulled the trigger of his pistol and blew his own head off.

*

FROM THE REUTERS news agency, August 2010:

> 'A GERMAN bank robber led his pursuers straight to him after taunting police in an email over their efforts to catch him. Authorities in the southern city of Wuerzburg said on Wednesday the 19-year-old

sent emails to police and two newspapers to point out factual errors in the report of his bank raid in the town of Roettingen a week ago.

According to the daily newspaper *Bild*, he mocked the police for getting his age, height and accent wrong, and then pointed out that he had escaped in a car, not on foot.

Police traced his email and arrested him in a gambling hall in Hamburg just a few hours later.

"He was completely shocked," the spokesman said.'

*

THE FOLLOWING COURT case made national news in December 2009 – and not just because the protagonist is a former under-16 billiards champion.

Peter Gamblin – who is clearly two balls short of a frame (or is that snooker?) – decided to mug a chap called Jonathan Franke, who was in the middle of a mobile phone call to a mate, one Joe Dale.

Mr Dale heard a voice say, 'Give me some money!' just before the phone went dead as Jonathan was punched to the ground.

He then re-dialled, and Gamblin answered.

Mr Dale asked who he was speaking to, and the idiotic mugger gave his nickname – 'Gambo' – and his home address.

Lincoln Crown Court later heard that this was because Gamblin, then 24, was 'full of bravado', and wanted to take his victim's mate on in a fight.

Mr Dale kept him talking for the next 42 minutes, as Gambo swaggered home. This might have been more of that famous bravado, the court heard – or it might have been because 'he did not know how to hang up.'

Either way, it kept him occupied while the police were alerted and made their way to his house to arrest him.

The whole thing earned Gambo a well-worn accolade from *The Sun*: 'Britain's daftest robber.'

Jailing him for three-and-a-half years, Judge Ebrahim Mooncey told him, 'You were the one who used violence. Your arrogance continued, you announced on the phone, "My name is Gambo, if you want to make something of it come to this address." And, lo and behold, the police *did* attend.'

And they made something of it.

*

THERE'S A WONDERFUL TALE on the internet about the cross-dressing robber in California who plastered himself in heavy make-up to make CCTV identification harder... but was identified by the lip-print he left on the glass exit doors as he ran into them on the way out of a bank.

Unfortunately, it seems to be apocryphal – I certainly can't find a source.

But it may well be based on the story related by forensic scientist Tony Tambasco to the International Symposium on Human Identification a year or two back. That concerned an unnamed armed villain from Mansfield, Ohio – where Tony runs the local police department laboratory – who robbed a corner shop. This creep was, indeed, identified by the prints made by his lips as he ran smack into the exit door in his hurry to get out of the place with his spoils.

He confessed to the offence when caught and presented with the evidence.

*

IF YOU'RE A CRIMINAL, it's probably best not to commit your plans to paper. But if you really must, you've got three options when it comes to dealing with the incriminating evidence: you can destroy it, you can hide it – or you can leave it somewhere detectives will find it.

Hmmm. It's a tricky one.

When police raided getaway driver Jonathan Ochola's flat, they quickly came across his notebook, which contained the following entry for Saturday June 12, 2010:

> *Go Porsmouth ~~rbobrey~~ robbery happens.*

Porsmouth was 'Portsmouth' – spelling not being Ochola's strong point (he'd also had two goes at 'robbery', as you can see).

His target was a branch of Ladbrokes, where his accomplice, one Rashad Delawala, waved a fake gun around the place and ordered the frightened staff to hand over the contents of two tills – a meagre £500 or so. As they made their getaway, Delawala dropped his balaclava at the scene. This contained traces of his DNA, and that quickly led detectives to his house. Faced with this evidence, he admitted his part in the fiasco, but 21-year-old Ochola, from Dagenham in Essex, insisted he had been at home watching football at the time of the robbery.

One of the officers found the incriminating plans he'd written, at which point he suddenly remembered that he *had* gone to Portsmouth with Delawala for a night out – but that he had known nothing about the robbery. In fact, he'd been in another shop buying cigarettes and sweets while his mate carried it out.

A jury at Portsmouth Crown Court took just 40 minutes to find him guilty. Delawala was jailed for two-and-a-half years, Ochola for three.

'When we found the diary we thought it was unusual,' said Detective Constable Mel Sinclair. 'You don't normally get evidence like that.'

I suppose you don't normally get robbers as dim as Ochola.

*

THAT SAID, THIS book is packed with idiots, and Tommy Franks must be somewhere near the top of the tree.

He was arrested and searched by police in Crawley, West Sussex. The cops found 21 grams of cannabis, and a bizarre to-do list.

Crawley magistrates heard that the note read:

Sell push bike, go on the rob, sell weed, get a job.

A noble sentiment, that last.

The 19-year-old – who pleaded guilty to possession of cannabis with intent to supply – said he wrote the list as an aide memoire, because he was 'desperate' for money to ~~fix his PlayStation~~ buy a new suit for a job interview.

Iain Starke, defending, said Franks disputed the amount of the cannabis found by the police, but admitted he was supplying.

A Sussex police source said, 'To be fair, he didn't have much choice. It was all there in his own writing.'

*

SUSAN BARCOCK WAS another dummy who couldn't help dobbing herself in – this time *via* her own diary.

The 52-year-old worked as a volunteer at her local Cancer Research charity shop, where everyone thought she was one of the good guys, selflessly giving up her own time to help raise money for a great cause.

In fact, she was shamelessly robbing the shop by skimming takings and donations – and helpfully keeping a neat record of her iniquity.

Here are some of her diary entries, which were found by the police and helped land her a four-month jail sentence, suspended for 12 months, plus a curfew and a supervision order.

> *'Bloody good day at shop £213. Man brought bag of coins in – £75 for shop £35 for me, well I had to count it.'*
> *'A good day as far as I'm concerned. £50. But not so for shop.'*
> *'Good day @ shop for me. £60. So got money in bank for tomorrow & £35 to spend. Oh yes.'*
> *'I was in charge @ C Shop and it was a good day for me £91. Oh yes.'*

'Good day in shop £124, £80 for me. Oh yes!'
'Dead £37 for shop £15 for me hee hee.'

Not so much of the 'hee hee' now – especially after Barcock's ugly mug was plastered all over the papers.

She got away with over £2,000, and also stole thousands of pounds from an elderly widow. It was that low crime which first led the cops to Barcock's door – they were called in when the 78-year-old noticed money was going missing from her house and bank account. It turned out that Barcock had stolen £6,356 from her. And it was while searching her house that detectives happened upon the diary...

Martin McRobb, prosecuting, told Warrington Crown Court, 'When confronted, the defendant could do little more than admit to the police she had stolen this money. Had it not been for her personal diary entries, there would have been no evidence against her.'

*

ANTHONY GARCIA TOOK it further still, and had a detailed tattoo of the *murder* he had committed etched across his chest.

Garcia belonged to the brutal Los Angeles Rivera-13 gang, and had shot dead a rival, one John Juarez, outside a liquor store in 2004.

The police had no clues to go on, and later admitted that they would never had caught the killer – but for his own deep stupidity.

In 2008, Garcia was arrested during a routine traffic stop on suspicion of driving without a licence, and his photograph was taken when he was booked in.

On his chest was a complicated though childlike scrawl of blue ink. Under the heading 'RIVERA KILLS', a peanut-shaped man is shown being killed by machine gun bullets fired from a helicopter outside a branch of Ed's Liquor.

A year or two later, a sharp-eyed LA cop, Kevin Lloyd, was checking through various mug shots when he noticed this one and was intrigued by the detail.

He checked back through old unsolved cases in the city's Pico Rivera district, and came across the Juarez murder. When he cross-checked crime scene photos with the tattoo, he found that a streetlamp, a road sign and a string of Christmas lights were in the same position in both – as was the body. Moreover, 'Peanut' was a derisive term used by Rivera-13 thugs for gangsters from Juarez's Pico Nuevo outfit, while Garcia's street name was 'Chopper' – hence the helicopter.

Lloyd tracked Garcia down and had him arrested. While he was in custody, undercover officers posed as fellow gang members and approached him to ask about the distinctive tattoo. To their delight, he started bragging that it showed his first killing.

In 2011, the tape of this confession was played to a jury and earned Garcia, 25, a conviction for first degree murder and 65 years-to-life in jail.

LA Sheriff's Department Captain Mike Parker told the *Los Angeles Times*, 'Sergeant Kevin Lloyd's incredible observation of Garcia's extraordinary tattoo, combined with great investigative work, is one of the reasons why Sheriff's homicide investigators are known as The Bulldogs. Fate and tenacious police work brought this convicted murderer to justice. Think about it. He tattooed his confession on his chest. You have a degree of fate with this.'

*

PERMESWAR KAULLYCHURN barged into a betting shop in Walthamstow, east London, pointed an imitation handgun at manager Carina Goffe, and ordered her to take him to the safe.

She wasn't impressed, unfortunately.

'What kind of robber are you?' she scoffed. 'There are cameras and microphones in this shop, and you haven't even covered your face.'

It was true that he was missing that most basic item of robbery kit – a mask – so Kaullychurn fled in confusion and, probably, embarrassment. As he went, he helpfully dropped a series of letters and bills which contained his name and address.

But all was not lost. Kaullychurn had an insider working with him – his girlfriend, Saveena Dooboreea, was the branch deputy manager.

She turned up to work that afternoon as normal – though she left after 90 minutes and took £6,500 with her, which was not normal.

Detectives found the couple, from Mauritius, in a hotel at Heathrow Airport the same day. Kaullychurn – who had telephoned Ms Goffe at work to berate her for dialling 999, and to tell her that her two-year-old son was 'going to know about it' – was snorting cocaine at the time, and told officers, 'Life is too stressful here. Five grand is enough for a new life back home.'

They had been planning to fly home to Mauritius. Instead, they got 10 years as guests of Her Majesty somewhere slightly less sunny.

(Months after the raid and subsequent court case, I put 'Saveena Dooboreea' into Google and up popped her Facebook page, still listing her job as deputy manager at Coral Racing and there, on the right, was a plug for another networking site under the line 'See who searched for you.' I like to think that if Dooboreea had checked the site it would have come up with the answer 'The Metropolitan Police'.)

Under the *Daily Telegraph*'s version of the above story, by the way, there's the following brief but tantalising filler: 'A thief who raided a Poundland store in Sutton, Surrey, was caught on CCTV after he returned to wipe his fingerprints from the till. The thief took a handful of change on August 1. The police are still looking for him.'

*

KENNETH MORGAN IS ONE of several crims to have been nominated in the Press for the accolade of 'Britain's Dumbest Crook', and, in a strong field, his entry is not without merit. This halfwit was jailed for six years after leaving his passport, mobile and keys at a burglary.

As if that wasn't enough, he also left his abandoned backpack, with his birth certificate and a signed tenancy agreement.

And his mug shot – on a prison ID card.

The 48-year-old wriggled through a window when his intended victim returned to his home in Acton, west London, but left all his stuff behind. According to *The Sun*, 'an investigation by giggling police lasted seconds.'

Morgan later claimed the backpack had been stolen and planted at the scene by some other burglar, but the judge at London's Isleworth Crown Court called this defence 'preposterous'.

I'm not so sure. You can see why a chap might take his house keys on the job – he'll need them to get back inside his own home (burglars can't leave their front doors unlocked, what with all those burglars out there). But his passport? His birth certificate? *His prison ID?* Why take those with you?

Maybe the poor bloke really *was* set up?

Ah, hang on a second. After the jury took just an hour to convict him, it emerged that Morgan had 23 burglary convictions dating back 25 years, and had been out of jail for just three weeks before this latest bungled effort. An unnamed source was quoted in *The Sun* saying: 'He has got to be the UK's dumbest crook.'

*

FROM BRITAIN'S DUMBEST crook, to the world's thickest terrorist. Mohammad Ashan was a mid-level Taliban commander in eastern Afghanistan.

In April 2012, he walked up to a joint US Army-Afghan police checkpoint, brandished a 'Wanted' poster showing his own face and demanded the promised $100 dollar reward.

The soldier he spoke to, Specialist Matthew Baker, was obviously doubtful that anyone could be that much of an imbecile. 'We asked him, "Is this you?"' Baker told the *Washington Post*. 'He answered with an incredible amount of enthusiasm, "Yes, yes, that's me! Can I get my reward now?"'

Sadly, he was to be disappointed.

Even when their man was in custody, the US military understandably had its doubts, so it carried out biometric tests which confirmed that

the man in custody was indeed the Taliban commander, who was wanted on suspicion of plotting attacks on Afghan security forces.

'Officials have guessed at what the unusual details of Ashan's arrest might tell us about the state of the insurgency – its desperation, its lack of resources, its defiance of law and order,' the *Post* mused. 'But, for now, the consensus has landed on the singularity of Ashan's act, and the intellectual calculus that led to it.'

Which is an elegant way of putting it.

*

THERE'S SOMETHING VERY important that you must never leave on your own death certificate, if – say – you've just faked your own untimely demise.

As Hugo Sanchez discovered.

This story begins back in 2003, when Sanchez decided that he'd had enough of life in boring old Farnham, Surrey, and his boring old job working as a web designer for HMV.

So he notched up a series of huge credit card debts and took out £500,000-worth of life insurance, and in 2005 his tearful wife Sophie informed the authorities of an awful tragedy – her 57-year-old husband had died from a heart attack while in Ecuador.

Sadly, no-one could see the body because Hugo had been cremated.

Besides the life insurance policies, and the credit card debts which were automatically written off, Sophie netted a further £112,000 in death benefits from HMV, plus pension payments.

Not a bad little earner, all told.

The 'grief-stricken' Sophie moved to start a new life in Sydney, Down Under – along with Hugo, who was actually very-much-alive and not-at-all-cremated.

Where they might have got away with their fraud, had it not been for The King.

Back in the UK, a friend had tried to use Hugo's old HMV staff card to obtain a discount when buying one of Elvis Presley's CDs.

Given that he was dead, this raised something of a red flag on the store computer. The staff stalled the friend while the police were called; meanwhile, the friend – who wasn't in on the major scam – tried to call Sanchez. He got through to him, but the fraudster hung up the phone.

This surprising turn of events raised all sorts of questions at HMV headquarters and with Thames Valley Police.

Hugo's death certificate was sent for and examined, and on it was found something peculiar: *the dead man's own fingerprints*.

Sanchez was tracked down using the number called by his mate and extradited from Australia (where he had been living the not-very-high life, surviving on takeaway chicken and chips, under the not-terribly imaginative alias of 'Alfredo Sanchez').

In May 2012 he was sentenced to five years, after admitting 12 fraud offences. Sophie Sanchez, 41, got two years. They had to give back all the money, too.

*

EWAN MCKENZIE and Stuart Bryce were locking up their restaurant in Perth at 11pm when they were attacked by three men in masks. Mr McKenzie was hit over the head, and both were forced to the ground. The raiders made off with cash, vouchers, seven money belts and a tin containing more cash coming to £4,000.

But they left an important clue behind for the police – a sweatshirt.

And in the pocket of the sweatshirt was a map of the area showing their target, the location of CCTV cameras, and escape routes.

And on the map was a name: Hubert Kowalczyck.

Kowalczyck was a 19-year-old from Poland who was already known to police, and it wasn't long before he was arrested, along with brothers Mateusz and Alexsander Gawinski. At their home, the police found plenty more incriminating evidence, including £3,000 hidden in a wardrobe and some home-made masks.

They each got 34 months' jail and a recommendation for deportation to D'ohland.

*

CALLING THE POLICE if you've been burgled is a good idea. *Usually*.

It's *not* a good idea if you're Stephen Barton from Boughton Aluph, near Ashford in Kent.

Officers duly arrived to investigate the break-in, and while nosing around they couldn't help noticing that Barton's house had a distinctive smell to it.

They followed their nostrils to his garage – noting that the windows were, oddly, blacked out – and discovered a middling-sized cannabis factory inside, with 133 marijuana plants worth more than £30,000 on the streets.

Barton, a 54-year-old turf producer (yes, yes, he was expert on grass of all types) was jailed for 16 months.

*

THERE'S WEARING GLOVES and leaving no fingerprints, there's *not* wearing gloves and leaving behind your normal, hard-to-spot fingerprints – and then there are the magnificent, come-and-get-me fingerprints that 20-year-old Ryan Creber plastered all over Nuneaton.

This particular cretin's string of attempted burglaries began at two o'clock one recent April morning, when he found himself trying to break the window of a house in the Warwickshire town.

Casting around for a suitable heavy object to hurl at the glass, he spotted a pot of bitumen. He went on to break in to a number of properties that night, leaving police a lovely trail of tar-coloured fingerprints on doors, windows and various other surfaces.

Laughable as they are, of course these idiots cause utter misery, and even terror. Imagine how frightened his last victim – aged 79 – would have been to be woken up by Creber groping for the bedroom light switch in the dark. He left black sticky fingerprints on that switch, too, before driving off in the pensioner's Toyota Prius.

Police later found the vehicle and – stand by for a happy ending – they also found Creber: he was lying beside it in considerable pain, having dislocated his hip in crashing the car into a tree.

He got six years at Warwick Crown Court, which sounds a little light to me, given that the court heard that his disastrous escapade had occurred just seven weeks after he had been freed on licence – that is, freed early – from a five-year sentence for a load of other burglaries and an arson attack.

*

THIS BOOK WOULDN'T be complete without hapless Jamie Neil, the robber who thought that a see-through plastic bag over his head would make a good disguise.

The 41-year-old raided a Co-op petrol station in St Austell, Cornwall, with accomplice Gareth Tilley – who at least had the decency to wear a scarf over his face.

Up against them was a single member of staff, 20-year-old Kim Clowes.

Tilley made out that his concealed mobile phone was a gun and ordered the Kim to empty the till.

But the phone keypad lit up and, seeing the lights through Tilley's clothing and realising that he was unarmed, Kim hit the alarm button.

Neil responded by head-butting her in the face before escaping with several bottles of spirits.

What he obviously didn't realise was that his face was clearly visible through the transparent bag, and had been captured beautifully on CCTV.

Detective Constable Steve White said Neil was 'less resourceful' than his fellow scumbag.

In June 2013 the pair, who had both been high on prescription drugs and drink, were jailed for two years at Truro crown court.

*

THOMAS WILSON WANTED to burn down his flat after his landlord ordered him out after incidents of trouble and damage.

The 24-year-old began by using a lighter to set fire to a pillow case lying on a sofa, and within minutes the fire was spreading.

Unfortunately for Wilson, he had neglected the key element to any successful arson: make sure you are *outside* the building.

By the time he realised his error, the property in Southport, Lancashire, was well ablaze and he could not get out.

A courageous neighbour fought his way into the flat and tried to douse the flames with a fire extinguisher. That ran dry, but it had damped down the flames momentarily, and Wilson was able to make it out onto a window ledge, from where he was eventually rescued by fire-fighters.

The ungrateful bastard later went to the neighbour and punched him in the face as part of an effort to intimidate the man into not giving evidence.

But even that didn't work out well for him. Wilson is slightly built, and the neighbour wasn't: he chucked the idiot down some stairs, and sat on him until the police arrived.

The jackass got four-and-half-years for arson, assault and witness intimidation at Liverpool Crown Court.

*

TO BE FAIR to some useless criminals – not that I want to be – their misfortune is sometimes down to bad luck as much as stupidity.

That is to say, their basic misfortune can be blamed squarely on their decisions to rob, mug, burgle and defraud. But bad luck sometimes comes along, just to prove that the mysterious forces of the universe do have a sense of humour.

Take burglar Michael Harvey. He had every reason to expect the house in Ipswich, Suffolk, would be empty. After all, it was midday and the homeowner had a full-time job. Surely he was at work?

Sadly for Harvey, the man was on nights, which meant that he was home asleep catching up on some zeds.

Even more sadly, he was a policeman.

Hapless Harvey, who'd only been released from jail two weeks earlier after a 30-month stint for burglary, broke a kitchen window and snuck upstairs, but when he opened a bedroom door he came face to face with the bleary-eyed officer. The policeman – who was not named in reports – knew instantly what he was dealing with, and not just because seeing a strange man in your house holding a screwdriver generally means you're being burgled. He had previously arrested the scrote.

Harvey fled to a bathroom and then, brandishing a screwdriver, said, 'Don't make me hurt you.'

'You aren't hurting me,' replied the officer, coolly.

Then he closed with the burglar, took the screwdriver from him and pushed him over the loo, where he held him until on-duty colleagues arrived to take him away.

In his summing up at Ipswich Crown Court, Judge Martin Binning said, perhaps with a slight grin, 'It was a bit of bad luck burgling a police officer's house, especially one who had arrested him before.'

*

SOME PEOPLE MIGHT take the view that our courts exist to oversee trials dispassionately and fairly and, if defendants are found guilty, to pass appropriate sentences.

That's all well and good, but it helps when the courts chuck in a bucket load of humiliation, too. After all, humiliation is a deterrent. Which puts me in mind of Judge John Burgess, who told an idiot house burglar, 'It was a pretty cack-handed attempt on your part. It was noisy and you didn't get past the window. You were caught red-handed. I'm sure it was to do with you being very drunk, and that is your problem.'

The subject of this well-deserved abuse was 60-year-old Henry Clark, who was caught standing on a window ledge, with his head through the window of the house in Allenton, outside Derby. A chisel and pair of gloves were on the sill. When questioned by police, Clark said he had been 'going in to get a clock'. He was given 180 hours' unpaid work and a ten-month jail sentence, suspended for two years, the court hearing from his lawyer that 'he is sober at the moment, although he drinks on football night'.

If I was a Derby County fan I'd be on the drink every night.

*

MOHAMMED AMIN WAS part of a drugs gang. His role was to conceal the cocaine and heroin until it could be moved on down the line.

Rather than keep it at home – the 23-year-old still lived with his parents in Farnworth, outside Bolton – he checked into a hotel room in nearby Lostock for three nights.

He went home each evening, so that his mum and dad did not suspect anything, leaving the drugs, worth around £50,000, in the hotel room fridge… where they were found by a cleaner, who told the hotel management, who told the police.

More drugs were then found in his car. Amin got four years and eight months inside after admitting possession with intent to supply.

Robert Kearney, defending the hapless Amin, said, 'A simple sign on the door saying "Do not disturb" would have prevented the cleaners from coming in.'

*

THEY HAVE IDIOTS in New Zealand, too. Had the following plot succeeded, it would have been the largest drugs haul to ever reach that country.

The gang responsible picked an unusual vessel to transport their stash – the sedate P&O liner *Aurora*, largely full of elderly couples enjoying a retirement cruise. Slow but discreet: at least, that was the plan. But their choice of transport proved to be their downfall.

New Zealanders Tony Wilkinson, 43, and his 26-year-old girlfriend Kirstie Harris boarded the ship in England.

They might have blended in on an 18-30 cruise, but their behaviour on the *Aurora* seemed almost deliberately designed to make sure that they stood out from the crowd. Their stormy relationship led to drunken, public rows in the ship's bars, with Harris being accused of sleeping with another of the smugglers – an Australian called Ahmed Rachid. Openly snorting coke didn't help, either.

They were arrested when the *Aurora* docked in San Francisco after sailing from Curaçao, and six kilograms of cocaine with a street value of more than £1 million was seized.

According to one report, when officials tried to enter their cabin, the couple blocked the door while trying to flush the drugs, all 6kg of it, down the toilet. The door was broken down before they succeeded.

In sentencing Wilkinson and Harris to seven years and three months' jail in May 2012, Judge Jeffrey White said they were guilty of 'felony stupidity'. Wilkinson's lawyer said that he had become 'enmeshed in a drug distribution endeavour that proved far beyond his ability to carry through.'

*

SMACKHEAD STEVEN BAIRD really isn't cut out for burglary – or much else, for that matter.

In October 2011 he broke into a house in rural Kempsey, Worcestershire, at 2am *and proceeded to switch on every light in the place* in his search for valuables. Unsurprisingly, this woke the owner – the music producer Muff Murfin, who had a hit in 1976 with *Let's Do The Latin Hustle*.

At 70, Muff was more than twice the age of the intruder but that didn't stop him leaping out of bed and giving chase, naked, down the road outside. Baird, 34, escaped his clutches, but was picked up by police soon afterwards and later sentenced to four-and-a-half years.

As so often, this story has a funny side – and a serious one. For an idea of the impact of his break-in, it's worth turning to Muff.

'The distress and grief it has caused my wife is more than four years'-worth,' he said. 'It won't make any difference. He will come out in less than two and do it again. It's what he does for a living. My wife is very traumatised. She doesn't want to live here anymore.'

Worcester Crown Court heard that Baird has 62 previous convictions, including two robberies; he asked for a further 26 offences to be taken into account. His defending barrister told the court that Baird's life had been 'blighted by drugs'. This makes me wonder whether drugs are such a bad thing after all.

Of course, we had burglars, robbers and muggers long before we had heroin, crack or coke, which suggests that class A drugs are not really the cause of such crimes. Baird would be a burglar, even if he hadn't turned to heroin. The drugs just seem to have turned him into a more addled, much worse and easier-to-catch criminal than he might otherwise have been.

*

WHILE WE'RE ON the subject of drugs, I must mention the brilliant plan cooked up by Austrian drug dealers to ship ecstasy to Taiwan in March 2012.

They hid 34,000 ecstasy tablets, worth around £700,000, in fake tins of dog food – sealing them up professionally so as to foil any customs searches. Then they sat back to await their windfall.

Unfortunately, ecstasy isn't the only thing which it is illegal to export to Taiwan – it's also illegal to export dog food there. So the Taiwanese authorities sent the tins back to Austria, where they were intercepted by the police.

*

BOLA ADEBISI MADE news the same month, for setting a new drug-smuggling record at Dulles International Airport, Washington.

On arrival from Nigeria, 52-year-old Adebisi was pulled aside for questioning by immigration authorities.

She told them that she had flown in to visit her brother.

OK. So where did her brother live?

Er, she didn't know.

So, what did he look like?

No, she couldn't help there, either.

Not so much a case of failing to get a story straight, it was failing to have a story at all.

She was given a pat-down, and her stomach was found to be 'abnormally rigid'. An x-ray revealed a stash of 180 thumb-sized pellets filled with heroin weighing almost five pounds.

Christopher Hess, director of Customs and Border Patrol for Washington DC, said: 'The amount of heroin this woman ingested is incredible, a serious health risk and very troubling if these numbers become the new norm.'

The previous record at Dulles for swallowed heroin pellets was itself impressive – 100, or about 4lbs, set in 2011.

*

THE FOUR-MAN gang had it all planned down to the finest detail, police said.

Well, almost.

When Jose Moreno, Alejo Cruz, Enumerable Vaillant and Bernardo Paz – all in their late 20s or early 30s – set out on that fateful July morning, they thought they were going to rob a heroin dealer in Homestead, Florida.

Which is why they demanded the $65,000 and stash of heroin that they believed Jim Smith had hidden somewhere in his house.

The thing was, Mr Smith wasn't a heroin dealer – he was an elderly mango farmer, who scraped an honest living from a few acres of land with his wife, Ada.

The terrified couple – this is the only bit that isn't funny – protested that they didn't have any cash, much less any heroin, and handed over the only drugs in the house, Mr Smith's nitro-glycerine heart pills.

Unconvinced, one of the scowling scumbags snapped the clip out of his automatic pistol to show he meant business... but dropped all of the bullets on the floor and spent the next few minutes fumbling on his hands and knees to pick them back up.

Eventually, the idiots realised they had the wrong people. Still, they might as well take what they could, right? So they soaped the engagement ring off Mrs Smith's finger, picked up a three-foot ceramic lion and stole Mr Smith's car keys.

In order to stop their victims calling the cops, one of the thugs ripped what he thought was a new-fangled telephone from the kitchen wall (it was actually an electric can-opener).

Then they raced outside, dropped the stolen ring, took forever to get the car started (they couldn't work out which key went into the ignition) and finally sped off in a cloud of dust.

As soon as they were gone, the Smiths used their actual phone to call the police, but there was no need.

The four simpleros had got lost almost as soon as they have got going. They were looking for the Florida Turnpike, and the bright lights of Miami some 40 miles north, but took a massive wrong turn on seeing what they *thought* was a highway toll booth.

In the films, the criminals just hurtle straight through these, so that's what they did.

Unfortunately, it was not a toll booth.

It was a guardhouse to the US Air Force's Homestead Base, and the four muppets had travelled no more than 400 yards before they were halted by a posse of heavily-armed military policemen.

That was where their dreadful day ended.

Dade-Metro County police picked them up and charged them with armed robbery, kidnapping, and armed burglary.

Detective Robert Malec described them thusly: 'Turkeys. But dangerous turkeys.'

*

THE PROSECUTION DESCRIBED the following robbery as 'poorly-planned and poorly executed', and I don't think anyone's going to disagree.

Four raiders burst into a Money Shop pawnbrokers in Bromley, Kent, one armed with a blank-firing pistol. As they escaped, the gang managed to drop both the gun and the carrier bags that had been filled with £3,300 cash from a safe. They were arrested shortly afterwards.

They were given sentences ranging from five-and-half-years to 10 years for the ringleader and getaway driver, 28-year-old Clifton Thomas-Bassir.

*

ALWAYS HAVE YOUR escape route planned. It's a basic rule of burglary, and one that Mark Roddis learned the hard way.

He broke into a mini-market in Dinnington, South Yorkshire, one night in October 2011, making a hole in the roof and dropping stealthily inside.

So far, so good.

But then he carried on dropping – by now somewhat less stealthily – straight through the plasterboard ceiling, and into the store below.

That set off the alarm, and the keyholder and police soon arrived. To avoid capture, the dazed Roddis had climbed back up, and had hidden in the ceiling space. He stayed there all through the following day – making small holes so that he could watch the staff below. After 14 hours squirrelled away, and once the staff had shut up shop and gone, he dropped down to the floor again – only to find he that he had landed in a storeroom.

Which was locked.

The alarm went off again, and this time he was caught.

Sheffield Crown Court heard that Roddis, 28, had been driven by gambling debts to attempt the bungled raid. 'Given the unusual circumstances of these offences, I don't think there is any benefit to the public in actually sending you to prison,' Judge Alan Goldsack told him, handing down a suspended sentence.

*

MOTORISTS IN MANCHESTER are safer since the jailing of dozy crooks Damon Keegan and Aaron Wilhelm.

The pair were prolific and successful car thieves, with a haul including a Mercedes, three top-of-the-range Audis, a Volkswagen Scirocco and a Renault Clio. All told, the stolen motors were worth nearly £200,000.

What they were *not* so good at was keeping quiet about it.

Wilhelm, 18, even changed his Facebook profile picture to an image of himself posing in front of one of the stolen cars. In images recovered by detectives from mobile phones and Facebook, the pair were later linked to cars taken in raids on addresses all over the north-west, some of the thefts taking place after they'd been arrested and were on bail.

As if that were not blatant enough, messages sent to Keegan on Facebook suggested he was stealing cars to order. He got 50 months in a Young Offenders' Institution, while Wilhelm got 40 months.

In jailing them, Judge Martin Steiger was moved to comment that the posting online of cast-iron evidence of the crimes was 'a singular feature of this case'.

Singular as in, just the one brain cell?

*

TRICKY BUSINESS, ARSON. Just ask Amir Ali, whose colossal ineptitude prompted *The Sun* to pose the question (yet again): 'Is *this* [my emphasis] the dumbest crook in Britain?'

Ali and an accomplice decided to firebomb a pub in Crawley, West Sussex, which had got caught up in a drugs war.

Now, I used to work for the local paper in Crawley, and if it was up to me a fair portion of the place would be carpet-bombed. But not the pubs – never the pubs.

Ali's role in the attack was to chuck two bricks at a window so that his mate could then throw a petrol bomb inside the building. But the bricks bounced harmlessly off the glass, and, as he bent down to pick them up to try again, his mate hurled the petrol bomb anyway – regardless of the fact the window was still intact.

Ali was engulfed in the resulting blast, all too briefly, but long enough to divest him of what few faculties he possessed. In a blind panic, the 28-year-old legged it down the dark street and ran full-pelt into a lamp-post, which left him sprawled back down on the pavement.

He wasn't hard to trace, having gone to a medical drop-in centre just around the corner for treatment to his cut head and burned skin. He got eight years; his accomplice got away, saved by an ability to navigate around street furniture.

(This is well worth googling, as the CCTV clip is online. Searching for 'Amir Ali Crawley' should do it. I guarantee you will not regret it.)

*

IT'S HARD TO SAY whether Ali deserves the title of Dumbest Criminal in Britain, or even whether he's the winner in the specialist sub-group 'Dumbest Arsonist in Britain', when he's got Lee Sood for competition.

Sood also tried to firebomb a pub in the early hours, initially with greater success. CCTV shows him stepping from the passenger seat of a Mini early one May morning and heading for the Walkabout Aussie bar in Rugby. Out of sight of the camera, he smashes a window, then returns to the car for a petrol can.

He pours the fuel inside and sets it alight – an internal camera captures the terrifying image of flames skating quickly across the floor. There were two people asleep upstairs, and my first thought when I saw the horrific footage was that I was watching a double murder unfold, but happily the occupants were woken by the alarm system.

Less happily, for Sood, the flames also catch him.

Back on the outside camera, the 20-year-old former soldier can be seen running to the getaway car, one trouser leg already ablaze. Getting into the car – as someone slightly brighter might have foreseen – simply had the effect of spreading the fire to the interior of the Mini. It can be seen shooting up the street, the fire inside spreading, until it stops and the screaming occupants bail out and rip off their flaming clothing.

Sood was arrested at the hospital where he'd gone to seek treatment for the burns he'd received from, he insisted, a barbecue. Yes, a barbecue in the wee small hours, in Rugby, in early May.

He got four years.

*

HERE'S A FACT that you could be forgiven for not knowing. Petrol makes a good Molotov cocktail because it explodes, but diesel is rubbish because it doesn't explode (except under very specific conditions).

If you didn't know that, no matter – it's one of those little facts that will probably never be of the slightest use.

Unless you're an arsonist, in which case you really should be aware of the important distinction, as Andrew Price probably now is.

His motive for trying to burn down a pub was that he had been chucked out after being accused of daubing offensive graffiti in the gents' toilet.

Price regarded this as an outrageous slur on his character. The 53-year-old former pub chef went back to the shared house where he lived and set about making two Molotovs, pouring the fuel into a pair of jam jars and adding rags for wicks. He was arrested before he had a chance to use them.

'In drink, he fell asleep,' Bristol Crown Court heard in December 2010. But even if he had woken up, The Dolphin pub in Weston-Super-Mare, his intended target, was likely to have survived unscathed. The court heard that the bombs would not have exploded because they contained diesel.

Price, who had a previous conviction from 2003 for starting a fire in a Northampton pub, was sentenced to two years, half to be served on licence.

*

WHY *DO* PEOPLE want to burn down pubs? I've been to my share of rough boozers, but I've never wanted to set one on fire.

Michael Morgan tried to set 'The Club' in Congleton in Cheshire ablaze, but, as landlord Steve Ball later put it, 'People will always remember him as the clown on the bike who set himself on fire.'

Cheshire Fire and Rescue service released footage of the attack showing the 33-year-old simpleton cycling up to the Grade II-listed building in the early hours, armed with a drinks bottle filled with 90p-worth of petrol, which he then poured over the front door.

Seconds later, in full view of CCTV cameras, Morgan uses a lighter to start the fire, causing a blinding flash which sets the door – and his t-shirt – alight. The idiot is then seen peddling frantically away from the scene, his top well ablaze.

He was sentenced to 30 months in prison after admitting one count of arson. Chester Crown Court heard that he had a grudge against the pub after getting into a fight and being asked to leave.

Although no one was hurt, the consequences could have been serious because the next door house was occupied, and the landlord and his family live next door but one.

'I don't think he had a problem with me,' said Mr Ball. 'He just wanted to set fire to the property where the people he had disagreed with had been drinking.'

The damage to the pub, Morgan will not have been pleased to learn, was minimal.

*

IT MUST HAVE been heart-breaking for the robbers to set fire to their £20,000 haul – but it was the only way they could destroy the incriminating evidence in a hurry.

The cash was the proceeds of a robbery in which a G4S courier was stabbed in the arm as he delivered money to a branch of Lloyds TSB in Kirkby, Merseyside, in June 2011.

Two masked men grabbed his cashbox and then drove off with it in a stolen taxi.

They headed for a park where they broke into the box in novel fashion – by putting it against a tree and ramming it with the car, which they abandoned.

Then it was on to nearby Walton for celebrations, in what they assumed was a safe house.

One of the Scouse thieves was 19-year-old Michael O'Grady, whose girlfriend, delighted at the way things had turned out, texted him: 'I reckon we can go to Blackpool hahaha!'

Nothing like thinking big, I suppose.

Unfortunately, the police were on to them, and early that afternoon the 'safe house' was surrounded by armed officers.

Panicking, O'Grady and a friend, 21-year-old William Hunter, decided the only option was to get rid of the evidence. They tried stuffing some of the money down the toilet, and rammed some more up a drain. The rest they heaped into the bath, where they set fire to it.

It was a plastic bath, so that wasn't a very good idea.

Over to the subsequent case at Liverpool Crown Court in May 2012 and the prosecution, 'Smoke was gushing from the first-floor window. The bath and its contents had been set deliberately on fire. Unfortunately for the defendants the bath had caught fire.'

As the house filled with smoke, the dim-witted pair faced a choice of chokey or choking to death. Wailing, they smoked themselves out, straight into the arms of the law.

O'Grady was detained for nine years, and Hunter got 32 months for handling stolen goods, having been acquitted of being the second robber.

The trip to Blackpool was postponed indefinitely, hahaha.

*

IT WASN'T THE biggest drug deal in the world, but Christopher Williams still took care to ensure that it went ahead without mishap.

He picked a secluded village car park, and handed over the package through his open car window to the customer. Neither of them leaving their vehicles. It was all very professional.

So it can only have been a conspiracy of the fates that, at that very moment, the chief constable of South Wales Police, Peter Vaughan, had called in to the car park with his 17-year-old daughter, whom he was teaching to drive.

Mr Vaughan took a note of Williams' licence plate, and a mini cannabis farm was found in his attic when his house was searched.

He got a seven-month suspended jail sentence and was ordered to carry out 200 hours' unpaid work; £725 in cash was confiscated.

*

AS A NOTTINGHAMSHIRE Police spokesman later said, 'It was a classic case of wrong place, wrong time for these four armed men.'

The delightful group decided to burgle the home of an 88-year-old woman. Easy prey, they no doubt thought.

Except that at the time (8pm, November 8, 2011, to be precise) there was a policeman in the house, taking a statement from the woman in connection with another burglary two nights previously, in which a purse and jewellery had been stolen.

(Incidentally, if you think we're being unfair on the people in this book, think about that – an old lady of 88, burgled twice in three days.)

Even with PC Paul McAuley inside, the odds were stacked four to one in favour of the burglars, who broke through the front door using crowbars – only to be confronted by the 30-year-old officer.

'I was dropped off at the house so there was no police car outside,' he later said. 'I'd been there for a few hours, and was just finishing up when there was a bang at the door. When I went out to the hall there were four men standing there wearing balaclavas and holding crowbars.'

Imagine for a moment the terror the old lady would have felt had *she* been confronted by that pack of animals.

'It all happened so quickly,' said PC McAuley. 'We just stared at each other for a moment, not knowing what to do. When they finally made a move I went after them. The pack split and after about five minutes of running I managed to catch up with one of them and made an arrest. It makes me sick to think that four grown men can target someone so defenceless, and my only regret is that I wasn't able to catch all four of them on the night. It was all a bit surreal, but I couldn't just stand there and do nothing. I was in the right place at the right time, that's all.'

Thomas Murphy, a 21-year-old from the Nottingham suburb of Chilwell, got three years – nowhere near enough, in my opinion – plus this book's award for Most Cowardly Burglar. Four men armed with crowbars against one old lady, game on. Four men armed with crowbars against one old lady plus one copper, and they couldn't run away fast enough.

*

OF COURSE, THERE'S a reason why most burglars tend to strike at homes occupied by old people – and not, say, Pan-American karate champions.

The guy who broke into a house Manizales, Colombia, thought he'd got lucky when he found a bag, a laptop, a couple of digital cameras and some jewellery in a bedroom.

Then he found the aforementioned Pan-American karate champion, Cristian Garces, and realised he'd actually got *un*lucky.

Garces – along with a number of other blackbelts who were in the house at the time – took exception to the intrusion, and pointed this out to the thief in no uncertain terms.

By the time the notoriously violent Colombian police had arrived, he welcomed them with open arms.

*

SPORTS STARS ARE always a target because they live in nice properties stuffed with gadgets and trinkets. But they're also young and fit and surging with testosterone, so it's a bit of a toss-up.

Ask Carl Bishop, 37, who broke into a posh house in Formby, Merseyside. His eyes widened at the goodies within – but then he met the owner, the 6ft 4in renowned hardnut and Everton striker, Duncan 'Big Dunc' Ferguson.

Bishop tried to smash a bottle of vodka over Big Dunc's head, but this had little effect. The next thing he knew he was waking up in hospital. He was later sentenced to four years for trespassing with intent to steal, and 12 months for failing to return to jail while on licence (he had ignored a recall to prison to serve the rest of a previous sentence after failing a drugs test).

*

AT LEAST BIG Dunc and Cristian only had their fists to, er, hand.

Pal Nagy, a 43-year-old burglar, clambered through an open window at a posh house in Budapest, doubtless cackling at his good fortune.

The cackle would have died in his throat as he slid into the room and found a sword-wielding Olympic fencer inside.

Virgine Ujlaky, 23, was in the middle of a practice session, and was swishing her épée (unless it was a sabre, or a foil) about the place like the Flashing Blade when she caught sight of the hapless intruder.

Police arrived 20 minutes later to find Nagy pinned up against the wall with Virgine's sword at his throat. He had to be treated by paramedics for shock.

Virgine later told reporters, 'I wasn't scared.... It was good practice, as I have a competition coming up this week.'

*

THE THREE COWARDLY worms who tried mugging a disabled 49-year-old woman in Barnstaple, Devon, in 2011 also unwittingly picked the wrong target.

Tammy Gatting was returning from the fish and chip shop when she was attacked. She was hauled off her mobility scooter and punched hard enough to cause internal bleeding which required hospital attention, but she clung pluckily on to her handbag and gave one of her attackers the most almighty head-butt in the process.

'They were not expecting me to fight back,' she told Sky News. 'When I head-butted the robber I think I broke his nose, it was that strong.'

The trio fled empty-handed, one with a very bloody face.

*

THE ABOVE EPISODE puts me in mind of the fabulously misguided attempt by two drunken yobs to beat up what they took to be two transvestites one August night in Swansea. The two men who were the intended targets of Dean Gardener, 19, and Jason Fender, 22, probably looked like easy prey: they were dressed from head to foot in women's clothes, one in a pink wig, black skirt and boob tube, the other in a sparkling black dress, stockings, suspenders, and matching wig.

But how misleading appearances can be. The two men in drag were on a stag night and happened to be, by way of a hobby, cage-fighters.

A swift salvo of punches saw the would-be attackers sprawled on the pavement, and the cage-fighters tottering on their way on their high heels, one pausing only to pick up his clutch-bag, completely unfazed.

Mark Davies, defending later at Swansea magistrates court, said, 'You know it cannot have been a good night when you get into a fight with two cross-dressing men.'

Earlier, just to make the episode even more surreal, the pair had picked a fight outside a nightclub with a man dressed in a Spiderman costume.

One of the 'victims', Daniel 'Lights Out' Lerwell, later agreed that the hapless attackers had picked the wrong targets, as they might have guessed if only they'd known his nickname – or that of his mate, James 'Lion Heart' Lilley.

*

SOME CRIMES – SUCH as murder – would ordinarily be too serious to appear here, in what is supposed to be a largely light-hearted work, but I will make an exception for that carried out by 27-year-old Daniel Tesfay – not least because the person he shot dead during a bungled robbery was not an innocent member of the public, but his own accomplice.

Tesfay – a be-blinged idiot of the champagne-sipping, two-fingered-gang-salute-throwing, hoodie-wearing variety – fancied himself as something of a hip-hop artist, and went under the stage name 'Wolfie'. Offstage, he liked for some reason to be known as 'Murder Mike'.

Dense Danny would have been more apt.

In August 2012, he and 20-year-old Jonathan Barnes tried to steal three Rolex Submariner watches from a chap called Jordaan (with two 'a's) Williams, who was advertising them for sale at £6,500.

(At this point, it's worth explaining that Jordaan Williams' moral compass was pointing in the same direction as their own: the watches were fakes he'd bought online for £350.)

The ad had come to the attention of Barnes, who texted his mate suggesting that they 'rob' them, and Dense Danny thought that sounded like a good idea.

So he and young Barnes went to see Williams at an address in Croydon, Surrey, and when they met him, Barnes shouted, 'Let's do it!'

At that, Dense Danny pulled out a semi-automatic pistol from behind a brown man-bag, pressed it against the chest of the startled fake watch salesman, and yelled, 'Do you know who I am? I'm Murder Mike! I'll blow your chest off! I'll shoot you!'

Given that the watches were fake, and that a loaded gun was being pointed at him, it's perhaps surprising that Jordaan put up any resistance, but the Old Bailey heard that there *was* a struggle between him and Barnes.

Dense Danny then did something stupendously dim – he fired into the fighting pair, presumably on the basis that there was a 50/50 chance of hitting Jordaan Williams.

He succeeded only in putting a bullet into the head of Barnes, who died two days later.

Tesfay abandoned his dying friend at the scene, and fled into central London, where he checked into the Kensington Townhouse Hotel in Earl's Court, southwest London, under the name 'Yusuf Ibrahim'. He was arrested a few days later and was given a life sentence, with a minimum 30 years to be served.

Afterwards, the parents of the late and not-much-lamented Barnes, Douglas and Judith, said in a statement that their son 'took people on face value'.

'The senseless killing of our son has been like a bad nightmare,' they added, tautologously. 'It was partly this naivety which led to his death.'

Partly, perhaps.

It was also partly that he thought it was a good idea to commit terrifying armed robberies with a gun-toting klutz for muscle. If you live by the sword…

*

PAUL DURKIN – WIDELY known as 'Durkin Donut', because of the empty space inside his head – ended up with a three year jail sentence… and for what?

Stealing an alcopop worth a couple of quid.

He stumbled through the door of a shop in Billingham, north of Middlesbrough, disguised with just a tea-towel partially covering his face, and armed with a knife.

Teesside Crown Court heard in October 2012 that shopkeeper Abdul Ghafoor recognised him as soon as he walked in.

This wasn't a surprise – Durkin was a regular customer.

Despite this setback, the yobbo grabbed the first thing that came to hand – a bottle of a drink called 'PS7', with which I confess I'm not acquainted.

Then he staggered out. Unfortunately, he dropped the bottle before he got to sample its delights, and was arrested shortly thereafter.

If this doesn't sound the most professional of blags, that might be because 24-year-old Durkin had drunk an incredible 12 pints of cider and three pints of Martini and lemonade before embarking on the crime of the century.

At the time, he had only been out of prison for two months, following convictions for torching his mother's house and beating a teenager with a baseball bat.

In mitigation, his barrister tried to make a virtue of his client's incompetence, saying, 'He had not even got the wit to steal a bottle of vodka, whisky or gin.'

*

YOU COULD FILL this whole book with the weird stuff crims leave at the scene of their crimes.

Burglar Mark Williams left his shoes.

Why did he take them off in the first place? Well, while he was nosing through the bungalow he was raiding, he espied a pair of boots which he liked the look of. He tried them on. They fit! He spent a few moments parading up and down, admiring his new look, and then got on with the business at hand.

Of course, he forgot to take his own shoes with him when he scarpered.

'A pair of boots was missing, but had mysteriously been replaced with a pair of shoes,' Leicester Crown Court was told by the prosecution in November 2012. Williams' DNA was, obviously, inside the shoes.

The court also heard that 46-year-old Williams was homeless, and needed somewhere to stay.

Okay, I feel sorry for him.

It also heard that Williams had committed 221 previous offences, which is why the police had his DNA on file.

I've changed my mind about feeling sorry for him.

He was jailed for two years and four months.

*

Q: WHY ARE THEY called ram-raiders?

A: Because they're as thick as sheep.

By way of proof, I present grandfather and truck driver Gary ~~Branes~~ Barnes, whose escapade was described in court as 'like something out of *Z Cars*' – though it sounds more like something out of *Benny Hill* to me.

Barnes reversed his articulated lorry at speed into a jewellery shop in Southampton in February 2013, jumped from the cab and ran inside, grabbing nine Rolex watches with a value of £150,000.

Result!

He paused only to warn the shop manager that she would be shot if she tried to stop him, and then legged it back to the truck.

Barnes wasn't wearing any sort of mask – not even a tea-towel, or a plastic bag – and a passer-by who saw him exit the shop later remarked, 'He looked so smug.'

And why not? Once he'd made his getaway, those watches could quickly be converted into cash, and thence to all the worldly delights his little heart might desire.

Ah… the getaway.

Barnes turned the key, started the engine, made to drive off… and found he was stuck fast.

He'd been a little too enthusiastic in the 'ramming' bit of the job, and had reversed into the shop rather too hard. His truck was going nowhere.

Now looking slightly less smug, and possibly even slightly panicked, Barnes hopped back down from the cab, unhitched it from the trailer – which was left at the scene – and sped off as quickly as he could, which wasn't all that quickly as his vehicle was artificially limited to 56mph.

Meanwhile, the police had arrived at the scene, where they quickly saw that he had left them a sizeable clue – the name of a firm written in huge letters on the side of the trailer. And not just any name – the name of Gary Barnes' actual employers.

Not that any sort of sophisticated detective work was necessary to link him to the crime, because he was caught just nine minutes later, having got all of two miles down the road, after a brave woman police officer clung to the cab door and sprayed CS gas inside.

In March 2013 Barnes, 54, admitted one charge of robbery at Winchester Crown Court and the following month was sentenced to four years and eight months inside.

*

BURGLAR JOHNNY TAWSE raided the home of an 88-year-old woman – as you do – and made off with an interesting-looking bag.

Only after he had made his escape did he look inside to see what loot he'd managed to nick.

It was the old lady's colostomy bag and fittings.

Prosecutor John Probert told Cardiff Crown Court in November 2012 that Tawse, 23, rang his victim's doorbell in a distraction burglary. 'He tricked his way into the pensioner's home and rummaged through her drawers in the bedroom before stealing her colostomy bag rucksack from the sofa. His fingerprints were later found on the pensioner's chest of drawers.'

Sentence: 32 months.

*

THIS NEXT CASE concerns one man's unfortunate failure to do his homework.

Let's say you have the need for an alias.

When thinking one up, it probably makes sense to check your local police website – just to make sure you don't accidentally take the name of your state's most wanted felon.

Especially if you actually *look* like him, and almost share the same birthday.

This is a lesson learnt all too late by one Frankie Portee, who was wanted in Massachusetts, USA, for assault-and-battery and resisting arrest.

In June 2010 he was stopped by a state trooper called Driscoll for the minor infringement of not wearing a seat belt while travelling as a back seat passenger in a car. As a matter of routine, Trooper Driscoll asked for his name and date of birth. Of course, being wanted, Frankie couldn't give his real name… so he made up a name.

Daniel Atkins.

By a fantastic stroke of bad luck, there *was* a Daniel Atkins who was wanted by the police.

As soon as Trooper Driscoll tapped the false name into his in-car computer, he drew his gun and made to arrest Portee. The unlucky loser was detained after trying to do a runner and given four years inside.

*

PICTURE THE SCENE: it's February 2013, Norwich town centre, and we're outside family-owned Dipples jewellers – which is one of those stores where the main entrance door is in a recess, flanked with window displays full of watches, rings and the like.

Rocket scientist Daniel Hutton is out on a smash-and-grab raid, and starts attacking one of the windows with a hammer.

It takes some effort on the part of the 29-year-old dimwit, but eventually he does manage to break a small hole in the laminated glass. He reaches in and starts filling a swag bag with items from the display.

If you're not troubling the Richter Scale, intelligence-wise, this sort of thing uses all your available brain power, so it's no surprise that Hutton didn't wonder whether the staff inside the shop would notice the racket he was making out front.

Or how they might react.

How they reacted was first to lock the door and then to lower the very slow-moving security grilles which protect the entrance to the store outside opening hours.

Result: one thick thief trapped like a rat in their portico.

'I must say, I expected the gentleman to run away,' said manager Chris Ellis, in what must be the most inappropriate use of the word 'gentleman' in history. 'It must have taken 15 seconds for the grilles to come down, but he stayed. We watched it back on CCTV later and you could see him pacing about a bit while he was trapped – though he was still putting jewels into a bag, for some reason.'

Hutton was jailed for 14 months. All the £3,655 worth of jewels that he had pinched were recovered, which can't have been hard since he didn't even succeeded in leaving the shop with the loot.

*

TERRY COLE THOUGHT he'd pulled off the perfect bank robbery.

He'd kept his disguise on throughout, and the Nationwide cashier had meekly handed over a bag of cash. Perhaps having heard of the Daniel Hutton case, he even thought to warn her not to remotely shut the doors, prodding the thick security glass with his forefinger and saying, 'You'd better not lock me in!'

Doh! He had forgotten to wear gloves, and police soon traced him via the nice big fingerprint he had left on the window.

It was only a matter of time for Terry, mind you. He was a veteran of several bank jobs, and he always wore a fluorescent yellow jacket – thereby drawing the attention of witnesses who were able to help the police with descriptions and other clues.

He was arrested after Kent police found him hanging around outside a branch of the Chelsea Building Society, still wearing the trademark workman's jacket.

The 50-year-old was jailed for 9½ years at Maidstone Crown Court, after details of some of his other master crimes were heard. At one, in a Lloyds TSB branch in Chatham, he ran in shouting, 'Give me all your money!' before his scarf fell off, exposing his face, and he ran back out of the door.

A few days later, he went into a branch of the Halifax in Strood, but the cashier activated the security screen which sent bank notes flying everywhere and left Cole's bag trapped on the other side. He left empty-handed, but hit the Nationwide later the same day.

The fingerprint linked him to four bank robberies going back to the 1990s, and the *pièce de résistance* was when he abandoned his hi-vis jacket in a public loo. He had taped over a company logo, which you would only do if you didn't want people to see it. And you'd only want to stop people seeing it if it was a major clue. In the event, it led police to a tenant at the address where Cole was lodging.

He had been robbing for 30 years, had served numerous prison terms and was on licence when he committed these latest offences. A Kent police source told the *Times*. 'If every robber was as easy to catch as Terence everybody would be happy. He must be the worst bank robber in Britain.'

*

FROM THE CANADIAN newspaper *The Times Colonist* of 13 March, 2013, comes the peculiar tale of the bank robber with a need for reassurance.

He approached a Scotiabank teller in Victoria, Vancouver Island, apparently to carry out a legitimate transaction.

Then he mumbled something inaudible, which he then clarified by explaining that this was a robbery attempt.

The paper quoted Victoria police spokesman Bowen Osoko saying, 'He then asked the teller for feedback as to how the robbery was proceeding.'

After getting no answer, the would-be robber left.

For a while.

He returned shortly after the lunchtime heist and was spotted peering into the bank. The unnamed 39-year-old was immediately arrested, leaving us able to answer his earlier question: 'It's proceeding badly.'

*

FOR PROOF THAT honesty is not always the best policy, we go to Slate.com, and a blog about 'murder, theft and other wickedness'.

Dominick Pelletier went for an interview for a job with the FBI. As part of the recruitment process, applicants are asked various questions about their past.

He mentioned that he had carried out research on child pornography as part of a graduate school project, which might have been OK – it sounds above-board, after all.

But he then went further – much, much further – and admitted that he had child pornography on his home computer, and that some of it might be hardcore. He wasn't lying, either, because 600 images of children were later found on the computer. Pelletier even told the incredulous interviewing agents that he had 'inadvertently' created child pornography by filming himself having sex with an underage girl.

The result, as reported in November 2012, was that the 35-year-old pervert did not get the job with the FBI. Instead, he got 80 months in prison, with no possibility of parole.

Slate felt it worthwhile quoting at length the opening remarks from Judge Michael Kanne, and I can see why.

'Federal investigative agents will tell you that some cases are hard to solve,' intoned the judge. 'Some cases require years of effort – chasing down false leads, and reining in flighty witnesses. Others require painstaking scientific analysis, or weeks of poring over financial records for a hidden clue. And some cases are never solved at all – the right witness never comes forward, the right lead never pans out, or the right clue never turns up. This is not one of those cases.'

There's a lovely touch on the Reuters version of this tale, too: 'It seems that Pelletier left the interview room believing he was still in the running for an FBI job.'

*

MORE ODD STUFF to leave behind at the scene of a crime: your wig.

Paul Hughes specialised in breaking into gym lockers and stealing customers' bank cards, using the money he stole to fund his gambling sprees.

He was rather good at it, too, netting almost £29,000 over a period of time.

At least, he was good at it until he left his hairpiece behind, and the police found his DNA on it – an act of carelessness that in November 2012 cost the 45-year-old from Coventry a four-year jail sentence.

*

AFTER MY SOUTH London home was burgled one New Year's Eve, I called the police. In due course, around they came, and I noticed one officer dusting the inside of a window sill for fingerprints. While I appreciated the effort, I remarked that surely no burglar would be so stupid as to not wear gloves?

'You'd be surprised!' was the answer.

My burglars were never caught, but police did catch serial crook Reece O'Callaghan, 19, who broke into a house while the elderly occupants were on holiday and made off with, among other stuff, a load of jewellery. The victims, Birmingham Crown Court heard in May 2013, were 'devastated'.

At first Reece, a jug-eared skinhead, denied any involvement but he ended up being locked up for seven-and-a-half years after being snared – by a packet of Jaffa Cakes.

He'd stopped midway through the burglary to help himself to one – why not the packet? – and left a beautiful finger imprint on the box. That takes the biscuit, eh readers?

*

A QUICK EXAMPLE of how the knock-on effect of dim crims' crime can hit the innocent.

In a doomed and deeply stupid attempt to steal some electric cable, Richard Howells, 21, used a screwdriver to prise apart an 11,000 volt mains line at Blaenymaes, north of Swansea.

Screwdrivers, being made of metal, tend to be good conductors, but Howells didn't do much listening in his physics GSCE classes. There was a bang, a lot of sparks, Howells set himself on fire, and 1,000 homes were left without power.

He was later arrested after going to hospital for treatment to nasty burns on his hands, and, in May 2013, Swansea magistrates gave the idiot a four-month jail sentence, suspended for a year.

One of the many unfortunate victims of his idiocy was his own grandmother, who was halfway up the stairs on her electric stair lift when the power was cut. She was left stranded in the darkness, unable to move, for four hours before being rescued.

Peter McCormick of CE Electric UK said, 'To the untrained and uninitiated, substations are potentially fatal, and in the past our staff have discovered charred bodies in substations after similar incidents.'

*

IT'S JANUARY 1, 2013, and 18-year-old Jacob Cox-Brown drives home after a New Year party in Astoria, Oregon.

Having had several drinks too many at a bar, he clips several parked cars as he goes.

A crime he might have got away with – had he not seen to fit to update his status on Facebook with the following:

> Drivin drunk... classsic ;) but to whoever's vehicle i hit
> i am sorry. :P

CBS reported that Cox-Brown was paid a visit by police, where officers found that bits missing from his car matched those found at the scene of the cars he had hit.

He was charged with two counts of failing to perform the duties of a driver (I think that means failing to stop after an accident) and, in the delightful words of the police statement, spent New Year's Day 'lodged at the Clatsop County Jail'.

Deputy Chief Brad Johnston said, 'He had to figure that this was not going to stay private long.'

*

IT WAS A PRETTY pointless and vindictive crime.

Yobs had broken into a children's campsite building and generally smashed the place up. They'd let off fire extinguishers and daubed graffiti all over the Toc H centre in Adlington, Cheshire. In a slightly juvenile touch, they had vandalised a poster headed 'Garden Birds of Britain' by adding 'R Gay', alongside a cheery message: 'Thanks for the stay!'

They did leave the police one or two clues, though.

On one wall was scrawled the fearsome-sounding 'Adlington Massiv!' That was the name of their 'posse', and it was guaranteed to strike fear into the hearts of all krews in the Chorley area, and indeed through the wider Douglas Valley.

On another was an even bigger hint as to the identity of the main perp – the words 'Peter Addison was here!'

And, indeed, the 18-year-old simpleton *had* been there, as police were quickly able to establish when they paid him a visit (having found his address via Google in a matter of minutes).

Addison, of Heaton Mersey, Stockport, and his friend Mark Ridgeway, of Poynton, Cheshire, pleaded guilty to burglary and got the usual slap on the wrist – a conditional discharge in the case of the former, and 60 hours' unpaid work in the case of the latter. Addison was also ordered to pay £725 compensation and £20 costs.

Inspector Gareth Woods said, 'This crime is up there with the dumbest of all in the criminal league table. There are some pretty stupid criminals around, but to leave your own name at the scene of the crime takes the biscuit. The daftness of this lad certainly made our job a lot easier.'

*

WHAT WOULD YOU do if you realised someone was drink driving?

Mary Strey was in no doubt – she rang the police to report the offender.

The transcript of her call reads as follows:

> Strey: 'Somebody's really drunk-driving down Granton Road.'
> Dispatcher: 'Which way are they going?'
> Strey: 'They're going… er…'
> Dispatcher: 'Towards Granton or towards Neillsville?'
> Strey: 'Towards Granton.'
> Dispatcher: 'OK, are you behind them or…?'
> Strey: 'No, I am them.'
> Dispatcher: 'You *am* them?'
> Strey: 'Yes, I am them.'

The dispatcher asked if she was still driving at that point – she was – and asked her to pull over, which she did. Police officers who attended the scene in Wisconsin, USA, found the 49-year-old Strey had slurred speech and stank of booze. She said she'd had seven or eight brandy-and-Cokes at various bars in the area, and the Associated Press reported that her blood alcohol level was double the legal limit. She was charged with misdemeanour drunken driving.

Her cousin David Strey, told the *New York Daily News* that he was 'surprised' by what happened, but that it was 'a good thing' she had pulled over. 'It would have probably been cheaper if she'd backed off one step and not gotten in the car,' he added, ruefully.

*

YOU MIGHT THINK that 2009 story is a unique case, but it's not – or not in Wisconsin, at any rate, where drink-drivers do seem to be unusually honest/dumb.

One Saturday night in November 2011, Cody Schwoch, 21, called 911, asked for the Lincoln County Sheriff's Office, and turned himself in, saying he was driving his car drunk through Merrill, WI, and 'wanted to go to jail'.

And a few months before *that*, a 29-year-old called Amy Tabaka drove up to a deputy's squad car outside the Red Granite Bar in the same town at around 4 a.m. one Monday morning, and said, 'I've had way too much to drink and I should not be driving.'

He duly arrested her.

*

WARREN JACKSON WAS roped in by two mates who were planning a raid on a delivery of cash to a Tesco store.

The idea was that they would nick a Volvo, drive it to the robbery scene, escape in it afterwards, and then torch it to destroy evidence and throw the cops off the scent.

Would Warren help them by driving them away from that point – in return for a share of the ill-gotten gains?

Why, of course he would!

He had just the vehicle, too – a Ford Transit van.

The crime went like a dream, until police started getting calls from members of the public who had seen the robbers abandon their stolen Volvo and get into a van which was handily emblazoned *with Warren Jackson's own name and contact details*.

The 36-year-old was jailed for seven years at Stoke-on-Trent Crown Court in June 2012 for his part in the £13,000 robbery.

After the court case, Detective Sergeant Phil Bryan described the plan as 'sophisticated'.

Which it was, but for one teensy-weensy oversight.

*

IF YOU'RE GOING to court over a restraining order (which has been taken out, incidentally, by your mum), it's probably best not to wear a coat with 32 bags of weed in the pockets – especially if there are several outstanding warrants for your arrest.

It's just not a smart idea. But then, Marquis Diggs is not a smart man.

As soon as he arrived at the New Jersey court in December 2012, he was nicked and searched, and the drugs were immediately found.

The 29-year-old was carted off to prison, where he has quite a few years to reflect on his own dimness.

*

THERE ARE SOME things you should not attempt with a broken leg.

Armed robbery, for instance. It gets in the way of the escaping-afterwards bit.

Waving a five-inch kitchen knife about the place, Kevin Nellis held up a security guard outside the Andersonstown branch of the Northern Bank in Belfast.

The first part of the robbery went well – the guard handed over the cash box.

The second part – not so much.

Nellis, 34, now had to hop away with his loot.

Unsurprisingly, he didn't get far. He fell over a few yards from the scene and, reported the *Belfast Telegraph* in December 2012, 'was easily detained'.

'Amateurish in its planning and its execution,' sniffed Belfast Recorder Judge David McFarland, sending Nellis down for six years.

*

AS GETAWAY VEHICLES go, mind you, you surely can't get much more farcical than a wheelchair.

Noemi Duchene was pushed to the jewellery store in El Paso, Texas, by her accomplice Luis Del Castillo in October 2010.

Then she got up, put a black plastic bin liner with two holes for her eyes over her head, waddled inside, pulled out a 12-inch hunting knife and demanded 'everything'.

Owner Linda Bradley refused to be cowed, saying later, 'I knew I could outrun her, because she was obviously not very quick. You cannot be terrified when someone cannot run and has a black bag on their head.'

Linda grabbed a stun gun and began chasing the 44-year-old Duchene around the shop – 'it was like the Keystone cops' – and as the robber made a break for the door a customer grabbed her and wrestled her to the ground, which is where she still was when the police arrived. Castillo, 45, was nicked outside, waiting patiently by the getaway wheelchair.

'The stupidest hold-up in history,' suggested *The Daily Mail*, and one online commenter summed up the case: 'Another success for the Texas school system.'

*

JASON BOLTON AND James Unick had a cunning plan – acquire a skeleton key and use it to steal the cash from condom machines.

It worked like a dream – within no time at all, they had hit 61 places across the north-west and Midlands, and were £4,658 up.

Their last foray was with a machine at a Premier Inn hotel in Derby – which is where the stupid kicked in.

Having nicked all the money, they decided to call it a night and booked themselves a room.

The following morning, two things happened.

The first was that the hotel staff noticed that their condom machine had been looted.

The second was that Bolton and Unick went to settle their bill – *with two big handfuls of pound coins*.

Helpfully, the pair – from Kilmarnock, in Scotland – planned their route using a satnav, which provided the police with a nice record of where they'd been, and when.

Bolton, 29, and 24-year-old Unick admitted six counts of theft and one charge of going equipped to steal, and were jailed for a year and six months, respectively.

*

THERE'S A PLEASING symmetry to this next yarn about a great piece of evidence being handed to the police on a plate.

Paul Brister, 33, was a serial flasher in Leeds, and often used his bicycle to make good his escape.

But the police stepped up patrols on his patch and, having spotted the perv around 8 o'clock one morning, gave chase.

Brister got away but had to abandon his mountain bike, which was left leaning against a tree.

Having targeted so many women, ironically it was now a woman who ensured his downfall – and not just *any* woman, but his own girlfriend.

When he pitched up back as home *sans* bike, she asked where it was. He told her it had been stolen, and left it at that. But she reported the 'theft' to the police, and as the bobby was writing down the details he noticed that it resembled the cycle which had been recovered from the scene of the last flashing. He then asked for the owner's description, and when it, too, matched the description of the flasher Brister was arrested.

Brister, who told a probation officer that he exposed himself because he was proud of his body, was given a three-year community order and told to attend a sex offender treatment programme. He'll be on the Sex Offenders' Register for seven years, too. Judge Tom Bayliss told him at the hearing in February 2013, 'It is not a victimless crime when people are exposed to this.'

And they say that judges have no sense of humour.

*

IN MY DAY job as the *Daily Mirror*'s investigations editor, I cover a lot of scams.

One of them involved a gang from Kent who ran a 'boiler room' fraud.

A bit of background. Boiler rooms involve crooks trying to sell bogus investments to innocent members of the public.

They typically start by obtaining lists of folks who have bought genuine shares in stock market-quoted companies, and then telephone them to offer their get-rich-quick schemes.

These might involve shares in non-existent companies, or fine wines that are apparently just about to shoot up in value. Recently, they've been flogging trendy green investments called carbon credits, farmland in Africa, and 'rare earth metals' that are essential for making mobile phones and computers.

If the first call doesn't work, they'll call again.

And again.

These people are horribly tenacious, and their sales scripts are honed to deal with every possible reason that the target might give for not investing. Most people resist them but some – often less streetwise, elderly victims – end up giving in. The result is always the same: the crooks disappear, and the punter is left with nothing.

Now, the scam at the centre of this particular case is known as 'land-banking'.

Two firms, Countrywide Land Holdings and Regional Land, flogged plots of fields as investment opportunities, saying that the value would rocket because they'd get planning permission for development.

Of course, there was never any attempt to get planning permission – and if there had been they would have failed, because these were green belt sites.

To give you an idea of the maths, one of their sites was a field in West Malling, Kent. They bought it for £80,000 and divided it, on paper, into 220 supposedly house-sized plots.

The plots were worthless but the victims that the gang cold called and bullied and lied to were flogged the plots for £10,000 each.

The tactics helped the scammers to rake millions of pounds, and the main culprits fled to northern Cyprus – which makes them, as the judge said, 'grotesque, cynical, and merciless', but not stupid, as extradition from that country is not a foregone conclusion.

However, the four they left behind to face the music weren't so sharp. Three were found guilty in March 2013 at Southwark Crown Court of conspiracy to defraud, while a fourth admitted the charge. I attended court to watch them being sentenced to between six-and-a-half and seven-and-a-half years in jail. It was payback time, and I was in happy mood.

The gist of their defence had been that they were just lowly salesmen who knew nothing of the wider fraud.

Which brings us to the stupidity.

Firstly, humble worker bees don't use fake names, and they don't leave photos lying around showing themselves with the key players on a 'works outing' to Monaco, thereby proving that they *were* part of the inner circle. But the part I liked best was the bit that earned a guilty verdict for 29-year-old Daniel Webster of Bromley, Kent.

In this sordid world there are 'openers', who make the initial cold call to victims, and who *can* fairly claim to be at the bottom of the food chain, and there are the much more senior 'closers', who have the vital, and tricky, job of converting an initial expression of interest into a client signing over their savings.

Closers are in the inner circle – more ruthless, more experienced and vastly better-rewarded – and Webster, despite his protestations, *was* a closer.

How could the jury be sure?

It didn't help that he drove a Ferrari with the licence plate 'CLO53R'.

*

THESE PEOPLE DO seem particularly prone to personalised number plates.

Working on another story about another set of land-bankers, I found myself sitting in a car with a photographer outside an office in Newton-Le-Willows, hoping to find the husband and wife team who'd been marketing plots on behalf of a company that had been shut down in the public interest, the High Court being told that it 'ought to have known there was little or no prospect of the plots achieving planning permission'.

But how to get their pictures? I had no idea what either of them looked like, and I couldn't even be sure that I was outside the right office, because it had the name of an entirely different business on the board above the windows. I'd also had no luck at what I thought was their house, a detached building protected by two sets of security gates. This was a couple who, with good reason, were making it hard to be found.

Then a Jaguar XK drove past bearing the licence plate 'P7OT BUY', and a few minutes later we had pictures of the conman in the bag. Not long after that, we spotted an Alfa Romeo Spider with the plate 'P7OT SEL', and we had his missus as well.

I also found a third central figure in the scam – surname Butt – in a village outside Gainsborough, Lincs, and he had personal plates on his Audi. It prompted the *Daily Mirror* photographer working with me to remark, 'If your last name was Arse, why would you want it on your car?'

*

FROM THE *MIRROR* of 17 September 2013 comes the following single sentence story, short and sweet (in more ways than one):

> A DRUG dealer was crushed to death by half a ton of cannabis bricks in his car when he braked during a police chase in Brazil.

*

DRUNKEN YOB ADAM Steff had something in common with the giant tortoise that he stole.

They're both on the slow side.

Steff pinched the poor creature – a rare Aldabra tortoise called Flo – during a drunken raid at Woburn Safari park in Bucks.

Given that she was the only female of the kind at the park, and was part of a captive breeding programme to revive her species, this really was no laughing matter.

Anyway, Steff flogged Flo to a mate for £30 – when her true value was more like £2,000.

The mate duly posted her photo on Facebook, where it was spotted by a member of staff.

Steff was arrested by the police after his DNA matched saliva found on an empty beer can he left at the scene.

In March 2013 the 18-year-old admitted burglary, and was ordered to carry out 80 hours of unpaid work, and given a curfew for two months.

Bedford magistrates were told that the tortoise would have died if she hadn't been rescued.

*

IN JANUARY 2012, the *News & Star* in Cumbria carried exactly the sort of opening sentence to a story that's likely to grab my attention:

> A THIEF who stole two security cameras left Cumbria
> police with one of their easiest ever investigations
> – because the cameras kept rolling while he was
> unscrewing them from the wall.

The rapscallion in question had burgled a charity called the Rising Sun Trust, which provides help for drug and alcohol users and their families in Workington. He hadn't been entirely stupid, in that he had begun by stealing the CCTV cameras in the backyard at around 3.45 one April morning, and had carefully hidden his face as he did so. But though his face could not be made out on the footage stored on the charity's PC, his hands could. One hand bore the word 'LOVE' tattooed across the knuckles. So far, so clichéd. But on the other, much more helpfully, was the word 'RAY'.

That just happened to be the burglar's name. (Which raises an interesting but separate issue – why did he tattoo *his own name* onto his hand? Was it in case he forgot?)

'It took police a matter of minutes to arrest 52-year-old Raymond Adams and charge him with the theft,' the paper reported.

Adams was sent to prison for 164 days after pleading guilty to theft, Carlisle Crown Court hearing how he had 109 previous convictions.

(No, that's not a typo: he had *one hundred and nine previous convictions*.)

*

I DIDN'T ACTUALLY know there was such a market in knock-off CCTV gear. Maybe it's a northern thing? Christopher Cummings spent four hours diligently unscrewing four cameras from the wall outside a former pub which was being converted into offices in Bradford. The building's owner, solicitor Amjad Ali, said, 'This guy must be Britain's dumbest criminal. He is staring straight at the camera – he is so close you can see his breath. Then, as he is removing the last one, he nearly kills himself. He was above a 12ft drop and he nearly lost his footing.'

Within hours of the *Bradford Telegraph & Argus* publishing the CCTV images, unemployed Cunningham, 22, was arrested. In July 2011 he was sentenced to a 12 month community order.

*

NOW FOR A BEAUTIFULLY botched hold-up in Dublin. The taxi worked just fine in the hands of a competent driver, something that carjackers Charles Deery and Dermot McFadden were not.

The pair had used a gun to force the poor taxi driver into the boot of the car before driving to a shopping centre in Dublin and holding up a security guard delivering cash to a post office. Even before the robbery, they should have known that this wasn't the getaway vehicle for them – it was an automatic, and they'd never seen one of those before so they had to shout back to the incarcerated driver to get instructions on how to work it.

As they fled, the cash box emitted a high pitched whine and red dye, and they crashed the taxi – into an Irish Army vehicle. The pair fled on foot and were found hiding in a funeral home (called, it should be recorded, Burke's). All the money, estimated at £25,000, was recovered.

Sitting at The Special Criminal Court in Dublin, Mr Justice Paul Butler displayed the sort of humour for which judges are famous, saying, 'They were effectively caught red-handed.'

Deery, 42, was jailed for 13 years, and 39-year-old McFadden for 10.

*

JOYRIDER CRAIG HUMPHREYS, a 23-year-old from St Annes in Lancashire, had similar trouble with the Renault he pinched.

Along with two mates, he pushed the car out of its drive, jumped in, and somehow managed to get it into first gear. But they got no further than the dead-end of the cul-de-sac before having to abandon it, because Humphreys couldn't work out how to put it into reverse.

Blackpool magistrates heard that he was unemployed (there's a shock) and gave him a six-week curfew and six-month road ban.

*

ACCORDING TO THE Royal Canadian Mounted Police, Brent Jameson Morgan tried to steal a Corvette in Prince George, British Columbia.

The owner had just used a battery charger to get the car going, and as he put the charger back inside his house Morgan jumped in behind the wheel. He tried to back out of the drive but, being unfamiliar with the transmission of a Corvette (something that you might have thought would have occurred to him before he tried pinching one), he just stalled it.

Then, because the battery was still flat, it wouldn't start again, and the electronic doors and windows locked.

While the owner called the Mounties, Morgan tried and failed to kick his way through the windows, forgetting two things, as the local *Beacon News* pointed out.

The first was that he had packed a hatchet in his backpack to cope with exactly this sort of eventuality. The second was, as the police explained, 'He could have gotten out of the car easily by simply manually unlocking the door.'

*

THE FOLLOWING TALE produced something of a passing political scandal, including as it does a senior Conservative politician.

At the time, the Press was interested in whether Dr Liam Fox had been alone in his flat at the time of a break-in and, if not, who his companion that night might have been.

We neither know nor care; our focus is instead on the 17-year-old who thought he'd get away in Dr Fox's car in 2010.

He might have succeeded, too – if only he had known how to drive.

The break-in began in a sinister vein, before plummeting into farce. A group of intruders took knives from the kitchen and left them close by on a sideboard, presumably for use in case they were disturbed. Then they found the keys to Dr Fox's Skoda and the teenager got behind the wheel.

He got it started all right, but seemed to have had a problem with the driving and the steering parts.

As Camberwell Youth Court was to hear, he succeeded merely in repeatedly moving forward a short distance before reversing – a manoeuvre he repeated again, and again, smashing a dozen or so plant pots belonging to a neighbour along the way. Eventually, he gave up and left on foot.

'Obviously incompetent' is how the court heard his driving described. Being a defendant in a youth court means that the idiot cannot be identified but, unless I'm being far too cynical, I don't think it will be long before he appears before an adult court where he can be named.

*

HADI MOHAMMED HAD failed his driving test five times and, to be fair to him, at least had the intelligence to realise that driving was not his forte.

So he got a pal, Derbas Hamed, to sit his driving test for him – but he failed too.

In fact, Gloucester Crown Court heard in August 2011, that despite actually being a qualified driver, the 25-year-old Hamed failed 'in spectacular fashion', making 16 errors.

He had an unusual defence, claiming that he failed *deliberately* because he knew that what he was doing was wrong.

Recorder Michael De Navarro jailed Mohammed, 28, for two months for fraud, and Hamed, who has a previous conviction for taking someone else's theory test, for three months.

All standard dumb, but the icing on the stupidity cake is this: staff at the test centre became suspicious that Hamed was not the real test candidate when they saw him turn up at the centre in his own car – without 'L' plates.

*

IN NOVEMBER 2011, two unusually dim shoplifters brought a little joy to the nation when, moments after stealing hundreds of pounds' worth of booze, they found themselves having to push their getaway car across the supermarket car park.

Rose Devlin, 59, and Denise Egan, 52, swiped £400 worth of alcohol from Asda in Chadderton, Greater Manchester, but then found they had committed a cardinal error when their Citroen ran out of fuel and they were forced to push it to the supermarket's own petrol station. They did at least pay for the fuel.

'Booze raid crims are total fuels' was the headline in *The Sun*, while *The Daily Mail* posed the question, 'Rose Devlin and Denise Egan: Britain's worst shop thieves?'

The fiasco became a YouTube hit after being caught on security camera in all its hideous incompetence, including the several failed attempts to shut the tailgate because so much drink was stuffed into the boot.

Incredibly, given the level of skill they displayed, the pair were not caught immediately, and might even have got away with the crime altogether had they not decided to try to repeat the stunt four months later at a different Asda store, when they were arrested and linked to the earlier crime.

But were they *really* so thick? For stealing booze worth £400 they got conditional discharges and were ordered to pay £280 in compensation. Who says crime doesn't pay?

*

A TRIO OF DRUG traffickers began with a perfectly sensible idea: get someone more stupid that you are to run the risk of collecting your illegal haul.

And so it was that Amjad Hussain and Sajad and Ajmal Aziz employed the services of Ibrar Hussain to collect a stash of heroin and ecstasy from a German lorry driver who had brought it from Holland to Dunstable, in Bedfordshire.

Ibrar was stupid enough to agree to the task; unfortunately, he was also too stupid to carry it out properly.

He put the wrong address into his SatNav and never made the rendezvous, getting lost and eventually giving up in a village called Harlington about six miles away.

That forced the ringleaders to do their own dirty work and, because they were being watched by police, get caught.

Gerry Smyth of the Serious Organised Crime Agency said in April 2012, 'Criminals like Amjad Hussain, Sajad and Ajmal Aziz thought they were being clever by attempting to distance themselves from the drugs. They were wrong. These men had only been released from prison a few months previously and not only have they lost their freedom again, but now SOCA will go after their drug-trafficking profits.'

*

ROBERT 'LIL ELVIS' SEGURA is a 51-year-old Elvis impersonator from Mesa Junction in Colorado. Early one April morning in 2010, he was attacked in his own home by two masked men armed with a knife and a sword. One of them was 20-year-old Anthony Gonzales.

He had worn a mask which covered his eyes. So far, so sensible.

Unfortunately, he didn't think to cover up the two distinctive tattoos on his face.

Below his lower lip there was '13' in the shape of a goatee; and where you might expect to find a moustache was written 'East Side', in fancy, gothic script.

Not the sort of thing you see every day, and indeed police told the *Pueblo Chieftain* newspaper that Gonzales, a known gang member who'd previously done time, was the only chap they knew with such eccentric facial art.

'It's hard to miss him,' said Sergeant Eric Bravo.

He wasn't hard to find, either. At the time of his arrest, Gonzales was already inside Pueblo County Jail on unrelated charges of contempt of court for possession of a controlled substance and a weapon.

*

SERIAL BURGLAR AND junkie Michael White was also caught out by his tattoos, along with distinctive scars, on his hands, but, unlike Adams, White used his *own* camera to provide the fateful images that led to him being jailed for 16 months.

White came up with what he thought was a cracking scheme. He found out the location of a safe in the office section of a branch of Starbucks. Then, while the staff were busy serving customers, he sneaked into the office and placed a covert camera disguised as a pen in a position where it was pointing at the safe. The idea was that it would film the staff unlocking the safe, and so obtain the combination so that later on he could come back and steal the contents. Brilliant!

Unfortunately for the 38-year-old, he was caught in the area, which is out-of-bounds to customers, and marched out of the coffee shop by the staff, who then discovered the pen. On its memory stick was footage of the thief's own, idiosyncratically-inked hand as he placed the pen in position.

'A clumsy, ill-thought out offence,' was how his lawyer described it to Sheffield Crown Court in April 2012, adding that the mechanics of the safe made it 'highly unlikely' that the plan would have succeeded anyway.

*

THERE'S A SCENE in the Woody Allen film *Take The Money And Run* in which his character, Virgil, tries to hold up a bank, only for the teller to pick him up on the poor handwriting on his demand note. Virgil is forced to explain the crucial sentence.

'I'm pointing a gun at you,' the would-be robber mutters.

Bank Teller: 'It looks like "gub"… That does not look like "gun".'

Virgil: 'No, it's "gun".'

Banker Teller: 'No it's "gub". See, that's a "b".'

Virgil: 'No, it's an "n", it's g, u, n… gun.'

And later...

Bank Teller: 'Oh, I see, this is a hold-up.'

Virgil: 'Yes.'

Bank Teller: 'May I see your gun?'

The scene gets better and better as ever more bank staff, unperturbed by the fact there's a guy with a revolver in their branch, quibble over the note. But surely it could not be mirrored in reality?

Normally, there's no degree of criminal stupidity that I would find implausible, but when I heard in late 2011 about a would-be bank robber whose demand note was so poorly written that it could not be read, I wondered if this was a case of a film morphing into a rumour that morphed into an online myth.

I was particularly suspicious, because the blog where I first read the short story was written in a state at the other end of America from where the incident supposedly took place. But it did name the bank concerned, so I sent an email asking if they'd confirm whether the episode was fact or fiction.

I did not mean my question to make light of what must have been a very unpleasant experience, however funny in hindsight, but I fear that's how it may have been read, because the reply that I received from Stephanie Heist (no, I haven't made up the surname), vice president in charge of communications at WSFS Bank in Wilmington, Delaware, simply read: 'Hi, Andrew – this is not an online myth.'

I asked her for some more detail – where and when did the attempted robbery occur? Can you describe the note demanding money? Could any of it be read? If the note could not be deciphered, how does anyone know that it was a demand for money? Was the robber armed?

Stephanie pointed me to an article in the local *Dover Post* newspaper, illustrated with a picture of the alleged illiterate robber – a white, balding, unshaven man in a black hoodie looking not unlike Bruce Willis. The report turned out to be almost a verbatim copy of the press release from Delaware State Police which confirmed the story and read as follows: 'Delaware State Troopers have arrested Thomas J. Love 40 of New Castle, DE, in connection with the attempted robbery of a WSFS Bank that occurred over the weekend. The incident occurred on Saturday, October 8, 2011, at approximately 2:50pm as Defendant Thomas J. Love entered the WSFS Bank in the Crossroads Shopping Center. Love approached the 46-year-old bank teller and presented a demand note written on a deposit slip. After receiving the note, the teller could not decipher what Love had written and handed it back to him, and asked that he rewrite it so that it could be re-read.'

In fact, the bank's staff only knew it *was* a robbery because of the few that *could* be made out, some appeared to demand 'no dye packs', in reference to the exploding paint that banks insert into stolen bundles of cash to thwart the likes of Love.

'Love then fled the bank on foot, empty-handed. A description of the robbery suspect was given to Troopers and New Castle County Police that were responding to the bank for the robbery. A New Castle County Police Officer was able to locate Love in the area of New Castle Avenue and Rodney Drive, and took him into custody. There were no injuries as a result of this incident. Thomas J. Love was charged with the above crime and committed to HRYCI [that's a prison] on $2,000 Cash Bond.'

Police spokesman Sergeant Paul Shavack was later quoted as joking, 'We had to call in the hieroglyphics expert.' He wouldn't describe the note to me because '(w)e cannot discuss details or specifics of the investigation as to not compromise the integrity of the investigation or prosecution', but he did add that the robber was not armed, with a gub or anything else (which makes you wonder why he expected to be given any money, even if the note could be read).

On February 22, 2012, Thomas Love pled guilty in New Castle County Superior Court in Wilmington, Delaware to Attempted Robbery Second Degree and was sentenced to serve nine months in prison, followed by probation.

*

THAT STORY REMINDS me of the tale reported in North Carolina's *Asheville Citizen-Times* newspaper, which reported how a man – his name isn't given – walked into a branch of Bank of America, picked up a deposit slip and wrote on it:

This is a stickkup. Put all you muny in this bag.

Then, like all polite robbers, he waited in a queue to hand the note to the teller. As he stood there, he started worrying that someone might have seen him write the note, and that the police could be called before he reached the window. Thinking quickly – or as quickly as he was able – he left the Bank of America and hurried across the street to a branch of the Wells Fargo Bank. There he again waited in a queue for a few minute, until it was his turn to see the teller. He handed her the note and she read it. Realising that he wasn't the sharpest knife in the drawer, she told him that, unfortunately, she couldn't accept the demand because it was written on rival bank's stationary; he would either have to rewrite the note on a Wells Fargo slip, or go back to the Bank of America.

'Looking somewhat defeated, the man left the Wells Fargo Bank,' says the *Citizen-Times*. He was arrested a few minutes later – *in the queue back over at the Bank of America.*

*

ANOTHER BANK ROBBER not fit for purpose was Anthony McNulty. He woke up with a hangover one morning in County Donegal after watching Celtic beat Rangers and decided to rob a branch of the Bank of Ireland – with a hairbrush.

The 48-year-old put socks on his hands and pulled a hood over his head in a half-hearted (and half-witted) attempt at a disguise, and marched into the bank. Then he pushed the brush, which was hidden in a bag, into a customer's back, and yelled, 'Give me the f***ing money or I'll shoot him.'

But McNulty, who's from Paisley in Scotland and was in Ireland visiting relatives, fled empty-handed when the manager Tara Rogers simply ordered him to get out of her bank. He then went into a bookies and placed a bet before stealing razors worth about £55 from a chemist. It's not really the same as a sack full of thousands of pounds in used notes.

Police caught him just 20 minutes after the attempted hold-up, and he made a full confession.

In sentencing McNulty to a year inside, Judge John O'Hagan remarked, 'To this day, he doesn't know if the horse won.'

At least one newspaper could not resist the headline: Daft as a brush.

*

ANOTHER ROBBER, ANOTHER weapon not really fit for purpose. Unemployed Darren Angoy raced into a Co-Op with attached post office in the Hampshire village of Marchwood, disguised with a scarf over his face, sunglasses and blue washing-up gloves.

He was armed with a claw hammer, which he used to try to smash his way through the internal glass partition dividing the shop. But the weapon, or its wielder, was not up to the job. Despite a dozen or so blows, Angoy failed to get into the post office.

Meanwhile, the staff – who were either terrified or bemused – had hit the alarm button. Angoy fled outside and leapt into the passenger seat of a black Audi which was waiting with its engine running, shouting 'Drive! Drive!'

Despite this dramatic getaway, the 23-year-old, from North Baddersley, near Southampton, was later caught and jailed for three years.

In mitigation, Southampton Crown Court heard how Angoy had lost his job six weeks earlier, split from his wife and suffered 'anger management problems'.

So that's OK, then.

*

LEE STREETER WAS already in trouble with the law in Staffordshire, having been caught with a drugs stash.

He was on bail, and had stored the mobile number of the officer who had arrested him in his own phone.

Time moves on, and Streeter, 29 and from Stafford, has a load of cannabis – 'cheese' in street parlance – that he wants to sell, so he sends a message to his mates.

In fact, being idle as well as stupid, he just sends out one easy group text – 'Got bone dry cheese if u need' – to all the numbers in his mobile's contacts book.

Which of course included the number of the officer who had previously nicked him.

He admitted possessing drugs with intent to supply and offering to supply cannabis, and in November 2012 was jailed for 16 months

*

IT WAS JUST AFTER Grand National weekend in April 2012, and the quartet of robbers in south Wales apparently assumed that the bookie's in Merthyr Tydfil would be awash with dosh.

They stole a Daihatsu Fourtrak and reversed it through the Coral shop front late at night, three of the gang jumping out (one of them optimistically opening the tailgate, in readiness for the anticipated great mounds of moolah), while the fourth stayed at the wheel.

It took a few seconds for reality to dawn. There was no mountain of cash lying around, but there was a safe, which clearly came as an unexpected blow.

'The men headed straight for the safe, literally looked at it, got back in the car and drove off again,' said a spokesman for the bookmakers. 'Nothing was taken, but clearly there was substantial damage to the shop. We keep very little money in the shop for this reason.'

*

JUDGE MARTIN RUDLAND has a nice turn of phrase. Here's what he told one idiot standing before him in the dock at Manchester Crown Court: 'You're a 34-year-old man. You're no longer a silly teenager and you're no longer a feckless young man in his 20s. But you are now a feckless man in his 30s. It really is time you stood back and took a long hard look at yourself. It really defies belief that somebody could behave so stupidly as you.'

So, what was so stupid that it defied belief?

Paul Lloyd, the subject of that thoroughly-deserved tirade, was a crook with a shocking record of previous convictions, ranging from burglary to dangerous driving, driving without insurance and while disqualified. On August 25, 2011, he was supposed to do a stint at a probation centre as part of a community payback sentence. Instead, he told his supervisor that he was too sick to work. And then he proved just how ill he was by forcing open the lock to a bike shed at the centre and legging it over a fence with a stolen cycle – all under the gaze of a probation officer.

Simon Barrett, prosecuting, told the court, 'He approached the supervisor saying he was suffering from back pain. The supervisor became suspicious and then saw the defendant climbing the perimeter fence with a bike. He was challenged, but made off. The supervisor saw the lock on the shed had been forced off.'

Lloyd was given two years.

*

YOU MIGHT NOT imagine that your old rags are worth much, but there's a huge market in second-hand clothes and, therefore, a huge black market in the same. I have written several stories for *The Daily Mirror* about organised gangs, usually from Eastern Europe, systematically stealing clothes that the owners believed they were donating to charity. Some of the crooks do it by simply taking the clothes bags left outside houses for genuine charities to collect; others are slightly more sophisticated and distribute their own bogus charity collection leaflets in order to entice householders into making 'donations'.

Rarely are any of the criminals quite as dumb as the following pair. In March 2011, police in Humberside told how they were alerted by a member of the public who had seen two men loading clothes donated to charity collection bins into a van in Garibaldi Street, Grimsby, in the early hours. Police arrived, and then the fire brigade had to be called because one of the pair had got himself stuck inside the large metal bin. He had to be rescued by fire-fighters using hydraulic cutting equipment.

'Officers attended the scene and arrested a man in connection with the theft of clothing,' a Humberside police spokesman said: 'They then searched the car park area and found a second man inside the clothing bin, which required fire brigade assistance in order to release the suspect.'

The two men aged 19 and 21, were arrested.

*

CLIVE WEBSTER and his brother Kelvin are not criminal masterminds, even by the standards of sleepy Ilfracombe.

They smashed a two-foot hole in the wall of Pedlars, a department store in the town's High Street, and Clive started squeezing through it.

Started, but couldn't finish.

At 17 stones, the blubbery bandit was too fat, and he ended up stuck in the hole. Eventually, the grunting 30-year-old managed to wriggle free, but there was little hope of escape – in the process, he had set off the shop's burglar alarm.

Not that the alarm was needed: 30-year-old Clive and Kelvin, 25, had made so much noise in smashing through the wall that half a dozen people had heard them, and someone had already rung 999.

When officers arrived, they found the brothers crouched below a wall at the rear of the store, covered in brick dust, with a screwdriver, a crowbar and a hammer. A ladder was leaning against the shop wall.

North Devon Magistrates' Court heard some fantastic mitigation from Clive's lawyer when the case was heard in June 2010. 'This was a wholly incompetent attempt at a burglary,' he said. 'In fact, were there a school of burglary, this example might be given to students on the first day to demonstrate what not to do. The hole made by the pair in the wall was just six feet away from a burglar alarm. Also imagine, if you will, the rather ungainly sight of my 17-stone client inserting himself into such a small gap. From every viewpoint, they were bound to fail. It was a misguided and instant decision, made only because Pedlars is so near to their own house.'

If I'd been Clive Webster, I might have wondered whose side my lawyer was on. Kelvin might have felt the same way, after his brief added, 'It was an inevitably doomed enterprise. Nothing was taken, and even if they had gained entry there was limited stock in the room they would have accessed.'

Kelvin was electronically tagged for two months, and Clive was given 100 hours' unpaid work. The hopeless burglary was apparently an attempt to get money to help provide for Clive's five children. Whatever he's got, let's hope it's not hereditary.

*

EVERY HALF-DECENT criminal knows that it is not enough to ensure that you don't leave fingerprints behind, but that you don't leave anything that might be traced to you through DNA analysis.

Antony Maxted isn't a half-decent criminal, though, so he raided the same house twice in five days and left traces of his DNA on both occasions.

Canterbury Crown Court heard in January 2012 how Maxted ransacked the downstairs of the house in Margate during the first burglary, running off with a torch and some random personal documents (I know, it's not much of a haul) but leaving behind a drinks can from which he'd been swigging.

Five days later, he returned, this time taking some stamps (an even worse haul) and leaving blood smears on a window.

The 42-year-old was traced by police through his DNA and jailed for three years after admitting three burglaries. He has 66 previous offences, and asked for another nine offences, including raids on a school and a doctors' surgery that netted property valued at more than £13,500, to be taken into consideration. My, how society's going to miss him.

In mitigation, the court was told that the father of two had been a heroin addict (naturally) since he was 17.

The summing up by the admirable Judge Simon James including the following, 'Hard working people need to be protected from people like you. Burglary isn't a crime against property, it's a crime against people.'

*

THE 2009 FILM *The Hangover* features a group of blokes who wake up after a stag night to find a tiger in their Las Vegas hotel bathroom. They piece together the events of the previous night, and it turns out that the reason the tiger is in their bathroom is that they stole it from Mike Tyson.

Life imitated art, sort of, when two drunk Brits on holiday in Australia woke up to find a frightened penguin at the foot of their bed.

Then they remembered.

The night before, they'd downed a litre and a half of vodka at a beach party before breaking into Sea World on the Gold Coast. After a swim with the dolphins and letting off a fire extinguisher in the shark enclosure, they decided to leave with a souvenir – a fairy penguin called Dirk. The next day they tried to feed Dirk, then put him in the shower, then released him into a canal. Thankfully, he was spotted by locals and returned to his home.

After being fined the equivalent of £640 in May 2012, the lawyer for Rhys Jones and Keri Mules insisted they meant no harm, saying, 'They tried their incompetent best to care for the penguin.'

Brisbane magistrate Brian Kucks told them, ' You could have found yourselves in a morgue if you'd gone into the wrong enclosure. Perhaps next time you're at a party you will consider drinking a little less vodka.'

But how were they caught? Because – naturally – they took pictures of themselves with Dirk which they uploaded onto Facebook.

*

I'M GOING TO DO this one in reverse order.

So, before the crime, the online comments from the website of *The Sun*.

'Add on 10 years for being such idiots.'

'LOL where is the video?'

'Its actually quite sad, i feel sorry for them they know no different. Shame.'

'These type of yobs are not THAT "hard" they ALWAYS hide their faces, just in case their "MUM" sees them!!! LOL.'

'Stick these kids in LA, they wouldn't last the length of their video in a real gang.'

Here's what happened. You've got five not very bright people from the St Pauls area of Bristol aged from 16 to 25, who think it will be fun to pretend that they're from the rough end of Los Angeles, and pose for a camera in hoods and red scarfs over their faces.

Kamari Lee, Narwayne Parchment (nickname 'Twizzle'), Linus Campbell, O'Shane Finlayson (seriously stupid hair, like a small volcano is erupting through both sides of his head), and Noah Ntuve set themselves up as the St Paul's Blood Gang (crazy name, crazy guys), and put films of themselves on YouTube – in which, imaginatively, they are brandishing guns and rapping in a strange hybrid which I can only describe as Wurzel Gangsta. Their rap threatened the rival 'High Street Gang'. What the Wysteria Avenue Krew had to say about it all I cannot say.

Funnily enough, this all resulted in a police raid, in which a .22 handgun loaded with five bullets and a sawn-off shotgun was found at the home of Parchment.

The jackasses admitted firearms offences and were jailed for between three and six years.

For final proof that society might just get by without this lot, at the time of their sentencing Parchment and Ntuve were already in jail for dealing heroin. To undercover cops.

Final word from *The Sun's* comments section: 'St Paul's Blood Gang. Wow, even the name is terrifying. I'm actually thinking of forming my own gang if anyone is interested... "THE CAMBRIDGESHIRE CRYPTS". Join me Monday night for some bad mudda flippin' knock-down ginger... Brrrrraaaapppppppp.'

*

WITH 25 CONVICTIONS for 84 offences to his name, you might have thought that Kevin Waltho would know something about crime – though I accept you might also assume he knows nothing about getting away with it.

He certainly proved that experience counts for nothing when he carried out an arson attack after he fell out with a friend of his girlfriend. He took some lighter fluid and set fire to a carport at a house in Stoke-on-Trent. The blaze caught hold, causing damage estimated at £12,000, and the fire brigade had to use ladders to rescue a family of five from the top floor of the three-storey house at 4am. We can all imagine what might have happened had the fire brigade not got there in time.

Waltho, 36, got three years and didn't even have the consolation of thinking about all that damage he'd caused to his nemesis's property.

He'd got the wrong house.

*

FROM THE LIVINGINIBIZA blogspot comes the short but sweet tale of the arsonist who wanted to torch the Fiat Panda belonging to his mother's former boyfriend.

But he torched a Fiat Uno instead, and then four more cars were caught up in the inferno on the outskirts of the clubbers' resort of San Antonio.

The police knew who to look for, because they had earlier stopped the culprit and asked him what the petrol was for. He had replied – with refreshing honesty – that it was for torching a car.

That had not been, the cops now realised, a joke.

The arsonist escaped with a suspended sentence.

*

TWO CRAVEN BUT unlucky teenage yobs attacked a pensioner as he was loading his car outside his house in Ilford, Essex, and then tried to force their way inside.

Michael Mather, 77 and wearing his slippers, was having none of it.

'One of the boys walloped me on the head with a two-foot log and I started bleeding,' said Mr Mather, after the attack in May 2012. 'They then tried to push past me to get into the house. I was so angry I swore at them and told them I was going to kill them. I went to hit one of the boys in the solar plexus with my left... Then, with my right hand, I hit him on the nose and it burst, which I feel a bit guilty about. After I hit him, the boys ran off.'

Mr Mather, sadly for the two would-be robbers, is a former featherweight who had sparred with Sir Henry Cooper in his youth.

'I've never forgotten how to throw a good punch,' he said.

*

IT WASN'T A GOOD idea, either, to pick on 55-year-old Eve Watson, and it was an even worse one to pick on her friend, Cane.

Cane is a Staffordshire bull terrier.

The robber came into her Bargain Booze shop in Torquay, Devon, in June 2011, adjusted his black hoodie, and said, 'I've got a knife. Open the till.'

Bespectacled and silver-haired, Mrs Watson said she was having none of it. Her assailant was armed with a Stanley knife, but Mrs Watson happened to spot a craft knife of her own on the counter, which she grabbed. Then she advanced towards the youth. She'd worked hard for her money, she later told reporters, and didn't see why anyone should just walk in and take it. 'I told him, "So you want to play with knives, do you?" We had a good old scrap and I think he cut his hand.'

We like Mrs Watson.

Despite her bravery, the robber managed to shake her off, and CCTV pictures show him ineptly prodding at the till computer screen to try to open the cash drawer. As he did so, Mrs Watson yanked down his hoodie, giving the camera a good shot of his face.

Then Cane put in an appearance and went straight in for the tackle – biting the robber, according to Mrs Watson, 'where it really can hurt.'

Three times.

He jumped over the counter and fled empty-handed. *The Sun's* headline was 'Crimecrotch!'

*

NOW, THIS SNIPPET has a lovely combination of stupidity and bad luck. Stephen Cole climbed over an 8ft fence to break into a building site in Ashford, Kent, with a petrol can and a short length of hosepipe. He was planning to steal diesel, but when he spotted the CCTV cameras covering the yard he decided to pinch a computer hard drive which – he assumed – must contain the footage of his crime. That's when he spotted £100 in cash, which he decided to take as well, by now forgetting all about the fuel.

It turned out that the CCTV footage was of such poor quality that there was no point in nicking the hard drive.

And the stupidity: what with the CCTV and cash, Cole had more on his mind than his mind could cope with – so he left behind the hosepipe, which carried traces of his DNA.

Thomas Restell, defending Cole at Canterbury Crown Court in March 2012, said, 'I hope my client will forgive me saying that he is not the brightest, nor the deepest thinker, nor the quickest to respond to common sense actions... And his short-term memory is exceedingly bad.'

Cole, 24, got an 18 month community order.

*

BURGLARS LOVE CHRISTMAS. The carols. The decorations. The peace and goodwill to all men.

The chance to steal all those presents, still in their boxes

One gang of three broke into a house in Erdington, Birmingham, on December 23, 2010 at around 6pm, and started ripping open gifts left under the Christmas tree to see what was worth nicking.

But not for long, because the lights went out.

They'd picked a house with the electricity meter that was just about out of credit, and spent the next five minutes falling over the furniture and groping their way along the walls to the front door before running off empty-handed.

'We were lucky the electricity meter had run right down,' father-of-two Tom Olner told *The Birmingham Mail*, after arriving home to find the police all over the house and following tracks in the snow while searching for the thieves.

What's the world coming to when you've got the combined brains of three burglars out doing a job on a dark winter's night, and not one of them thinks it's a good idea to bring a torch?

*

THE SUN RAN the following story under the headline 'Taxi For Stupid!', though I think it's fairer to put it in the bad luck category.

It concerns Jake Ormerod, an 18-year-old who broke into the house of taxi-driver Don Smith and stole a laptop and mobile.

A few days later, young Jake decides he'll use the mobile to book a cab.

He could have chosen any cab firm to ring, but he called Mr Smith's.

If that wasn't bad enough, he happened to get the one controller on duty who would recognise Mr Smith's mobile number immediately.

Instead of sending a taxi, a police car arrived to pick up Ormerod.

At Torbay magistrates in Devon he later admitted burglary and two separate cases of theft and shoplifting.

Mr Smith said, 'He must be the unluckiest burglar in the world.'

*

IF YOU'RE GOING to claim disability benefits, it's normally a good idea to have a disability.

If you *don't* have a disability, it's sensible to fake one – a crucial point overlooked by that class of fraudsters seemingly addicted to public displays of physical prowess. This is a special brand of criminal stupidity and, being parasites, it seems appropriate that the villains seem to have the brain power of the more unpleasant single-cell organisms.

The following story from *The Daily Mirror* in December 2011 needs no elaboration:

> A BENEFITS cheat who claimed he could barely walk was filmed marching along in a kilt, banging a drum.
>
> Alexander Clarkson, 63, was rumbled when he was seen playing for Preston's Scottish Pipe and Drum band on Remembrance Day.
>
> The ex-soldier, from Blackpool, admitted falsely claiming £17,329 in benefits and was given a 56-day suspended jail sentence.
>
> District Judge Jeff Brailsford told him at Blackpool magistrates court: 'There seemed to be no hindrance to your mobility.'

*

A FEW INVIGORATING rounds of golf seem to be a routine pastime for the 'disabled', judging by a string of court cases.

There was former forklift driver Chris Mowatt, caught thrashing around 18 holes – despite claiming he 'couldn't walk more than 25 yards without a stick' because of a slipped disc. He had pocketed a total of £15,888 – handed over by honest, working taxpayers and meant to help the genuinely disabled.

Valerie Lewis told welfare officials that she was a 'virtual prisoner in her home', could not walk outdoors without a helper, and needed assistance with bathing and getting out of bed. Despite this, she didn't merely play four rounds of golf every week – she *was the lady captain* at her £600-a-year club.

You've got admire her gall. The poor thing had stolen £40,000 in benefits before being rumbled.

Philip Bond played up to two rounds of golf every day, and managed to get down to a respectable 12 handicap (and that was his only handicap) while claiming £36,400 in benefits over 12 years on the grounds that he could 'barely walk'.

The 62-year-old from Torquay even took part in tournaments, which is pretty remarkable for someone suffering from 'severe breathlessness' and who apparently struggled to get in and out of bed. When he wasn't knocking a small white ball into (or around) holes with a stick, he was working as a painter and decorator. He was jailed for seven months.

Alan Bulpin was a bit more inventive than the 'can barely walk' crowd – he claimed he couldn't even bend to wash his feet. Despite this, he got *his* golf handicap down to a very decent six, a jury was told. Investigators followed him onto the links at Falmouth Golf Club in Cornwall, where they filmed him playing a full round and pushing his trolley for almost four miles. Truro Crown Court heard he had been claiming disability living allowance of £91 a week for 18 months before investigators were tipped off. Presumably by a rival with a handicap of seven. Golfers can be petty like that.

*

OF COURSE, FOR some, golf is not nearly energetic enough.

Retired history teacher Keith Walklate, 61, was caught playing badminton, and was also fond of mountain biking and visits to the gym. This was despite his claiming disability benefits on the grounds that – yes, you've guessed it – he could 'barely walk' following a knee operation for osteoarthritis.

Over a number of years, he claimed more than £17,000, telling officials that he needed his wife's help to climb steps. He was sentenced to 250 hours' unpaid work. If it was down to me, I'd have made him carry it out back in the history classroom – teaching children about the origins of the welfare state, a shining beacon that shows how, like every civilisation should, we care for our genuinely sick and vulnerable, and despise the workshy who exploit the system for their own selfish and lazy ends.

'Disabled' Shean Saunders, 34, went further still – much further. He played for Crewkerne Rugby Club while fraudulently obtaining more than £7,000 for what he claimed was a form of paralysis. After an anonymous tip-off, council investigators discovered him knocking seven bells out of his opponents on the rugger pitch, and later followed him to his job as a cleaner.

Clare Jones pocketed £891 in incapacity benefits and £5,125 in disability living allowance after insisting that she 'needed crutches to walk'; apparently, her back was so bad that she could not even stand at the cooker, or 'cut vegetables'.

But then the 38-year-old numbnut went *skydiving* from 12,000ft over Swansea Airport, and even paid extra for a professional film of the event – which chortling prosecutors later used against her. You can still see the footage online.

*

NOW, WHO'S THE most hated man at any football match? The referee, obviously.

So, no sensible benefits cheat would think of donning the black (more fluorescent yellow, these days) and picking up a whistle.

The odds are that you'll offend someone, and a tip to the Department of Work and Pensions will follow as surely as a red card follows two yellows. The consequences of that goal you disallowed, or that chap you sent off rather high-handedly, will be a court appearance.

Ask Terry Langford – a 62-year-old who claimed to be 'crippled with arthritis' and who said he couldn't even cook or dress himself. But Bolton magistrates were told by the Department for Work and Pensions prosecutor, 'Video footage was taken of him when he was refereeing, and he was seen walking 100 yards from one end of the pitch to the other, and jogging and keeping up with play. He was able to stop, start, swivel, and turn.'

Steven Paskin from Newport, Gwent, claimed benefits after complaining – you'd think they'd be a bit more inventive – that he 'could not walk more than 100 yards' without 'extreme tiredness and discomfort'. Yet the 46-year-old was a regular 'super-fit' ref at local league matches. Benefits investigators were tipped off, and Paskin was convicted of falsely claiming more than £17,000, and jailed for eight months.

Stephen Southern suffered, so he claimed, from severe chest pains and dizziness, and had an inability to walk that made Steve Paskin look like an Olympic athlete – he 'could walk barely 25 yards', even with the aid of a stick. Yet the 49-year-old from Wigan officiated at more than 40 matches in one season. The usual pattern followed. Southern upsets someone. Benefits officials get anonymous tip-off. Southern gets conviction. He got away with 300 hours community work. Something strenuous, hopefully.

*

WHO MIGHT HATE you even *more* than you hate a referee?

Your ex, naturally – which is how Tina Attanasio came to grief. She fiddled £19,000 in disability hand-outs after claiming to have a bad back that left her 'too weak to walk without crutches', and didn't think twice about letting her boyfriend film her shooting down a water slide in a bikini while on a French holiday. After all, her boyfriend's not going to snitch, is he?

But when they split up her ex handed the footage to investigators, and the 51-year-old from Cardiff got 10 weeks in chokey.

*

ACTUALLY, WHY *DO* these people allow themselves to be filmed? (The answer, I suppose, is in the title of this book.)

Gillian Hulme, a 55-year-old mother of two from Stoke-on-Trent, claimed disability living allowance worth almost £46,000 by insisting that she was unable to work because she found it 'too painful to walk'. But besides going to her local gym up to five times a week, she *joined her local running club*, and took part in 54 races.

Eventually, she was filmed taking part in a five-miler.

Result: eight month sentence – suspended. Maybe she wasn't so stupid, after all.

*

HOWARD BARON CAN walk just fine – though whether he can walk and chew gum at the same time is open to question.

Baron is an unusually dim benefits fraudster who claimed £37,174 in various payments by claiming he was living alone, when in fact he had installed his girlfriend in his flat in Portsmouth a full five years earlier.

But what's stupid about this? Well, he was caught by clear-as-day footage from CCTV cameras installed around the building, which showed him and his partner wandering in and out at all times of the day and night over a long period. And it's not like he didn't know the cameras where there – he had been at the forefront of a campaign against their introduction, claiming that he 'did not want to be spied on'.

No, er, kidding, Sherlock.

Baron, 49, got a seven-month prison term suspended for 12 months.

*

IYAN ARTAN IS in a dumb benefits-cheat category of her own. Her undoing was an astonishingly stupid act of greed – or maybe that should be a greedy act of stupidity?

The asylum seeker from Somalia had claimed £150,000 in hand-outs, and would still be getting away with it – had she not tried to rip-off a High Street store over a £3 bottle of shampoo.

She found a discarded Boots receipt lying on the pavement, and tried to use it to get money back for a bottle of shampoo she had taken from a shelf.

Suspicious staff called the police, who found £2,000 in cash in her bag, along with the ID documents which she was using to run her benefit fraud.

And that was the end of her racket – which had earned her the keys to two London flats – one in Islington, and another in Hampstead – and benefits for a non-existent child.

Jailing her for 21 months, Judge Peter Clarke QC said at Blackfriars Crown Court, 'One of the particularly disgraceful things is that you come to this country and take money when we are looking after your starving countrymen back in the Horn of Africa.'

Iyan Artan is a false name, by the way. Her real identity is unknown, but another of her fake names was 'Lucky'.

Up to a point.

*

SOME OF THESE people will stop at almost nothing.

After his father died, Christopher Blackburn kept the body in his home at Penwortham, Lancs, so that he could carry on claiming his dad's benefits.

It can't be easy keeping the decomposing body of your own father in a downstairs bedroom for five months without anybody noticing, and Blackburn's solution – *air fresheners* – just wasn't up to the job.

Eventually, the police were tipped off. I don't know who the informant was, but *The Daily Mirror* reported that 'Blackburn's ex-girlfriend had visited and noticed there were a lot of air fresheners and held her nose because of the smell.'

Meanwhile, the 29-year-old had pocketed almost £2,000 in benefits. In March 2012 he was sentenced to three years' jail at Preston Crown Court (and his dad was given a decent burial).

*

PERHAPS HE WAS inspired by the US case of Thomas Prusik-Parkin, 53, who appeared in a New York court accused of dressing up as his dead mother to claim her benefits.

He'd kept the charade going for six years, and had pocketed £70,000.

CCTV footage appeared to show him wearing one of his mum's dresses, a wig and heavy make-up to carry out the scam, with a friend acting as a nephew to help 'her' to appointments.

His mum Irene had died in 2003 aged 73, but he was said not to have registered the death in order that he could continue to collect her £430-a-month social security. Since that's what he managed until 2009, he wasn't that stupid, though his excuse was utterly barking. When he was arrested in 2009, detectives claim he said, 'I held my mother when she was dying and breathed in her last breath, so I am my mother.'

His downfall came after he got into a legal battle over his mother's property and was accused of filing a false affidavit. The matter was referred to the district attorney and an investigation began, during which Prusik-Parkin boldly – or perhaps very, very stupidly – told officers that he would arrange for his mother to meet them.

Although he had (amazingly) fooled social security staff, these experienced detectives saw through the disguise instantly.

'When prosecutors and detective investigators arrived, they found Prusik-Parkin dressed as his 77-year-old mother, wearing a red cardigan, lipstick, manicured nails and breathing through an oxygen tank,' the DA's office said.

They also now had proof that Irene was dead – a photograph of her tombstone.

They don't mess around in the USA. None of this six months' prison suspended for two years, and a weekend spent litter-picking – he was sentenced to 41 years in prison for grand larceny and mortgage fraud. The 44-year-old friend who played the part of the nephew got three years after admitting his part in the scam.

*

VAT FRAUD, LIKE benefit fraud, amounts to a rip-off perpetrated by a few parasites on the majority of law-abiding taxpayers. I had the pleasure of covering a VAT fraud case in Croydon Crown Court in the summer of 2011, and watched as the two culprits got jail sentences (one of them suspended), all thanks to a mixture of their own greed and stupidity.

On paper, Haris Mukhtar, and his brother and lesser offender Adam, ran a series of businesses, from chauffeur companies to jeans and rice importers.

They claimed around £1million in VAT rebates on business expenses, which might have been quite legitimate – had the businesses actually existed.

To give you an idea of how heartless they were, the pair also pocketed around £330,000 that was deducted in National Insurance and PAYE from staff pay-packets at one of their companies that *did* exist, and which should have been passed on to the taxman. That potentially meant that those employees would not get the state pensions and other benefits to which they'd normally be entitled.

It was not the simplest of scams, and it required the pair to use multiple fake companies and at least 21 aliases, and this is where they came unstuck.

The brothers were just not bright enough for such a prolonged and extensive deception.

Staff and HM Revenue & Customs became suspicious when they seemed unsure as to how to spell their own supposed first names, or forgot which fake accent went with which fake identity.

Haris, described as 'utterly bent' by the judge, got six years; Adam got 12 months, suspended.

Much of the cash was spent on flash cars; Adam liked to swan about the place in a Lamborghini – at least, he did until he wrote it off by driving too fast over a speed bump.

*

ACTUALLY CARS, CRIMINALS and low IQs is a combination made in comedy heaven.

Let's start with the basics: cars need petrol.

It's an important detail, but one that the more stupid elements of the criminal community find so easy to forget, which is why five jewellery shop raiders ended up being sentenced to between four and eight years inside.

The raid in Ilford, Essex, began so well, with Imran Khan and Abdul Said taking just 20 seconds to smash the shop window with a pickaxe and a sledgehammer.

Accomplices Sayid Mohammed and Adama Belle then stuffed jewellery worth £9,000 into pillow cases.

Everything now lay in the hands of getaway driver Mohammed Alasow, an experienced scumbag with a record of 25 offences including assault, burglary and robbery.

Tragically for the gang, the 19-year-old Somali had forgotten to fill up his Rover, with the result that it spluttered to a halt in the middle of the road in nearby Beckton – probably just as the gang of dimwits were high-fiving each other in glee.

There happened to be on hand a police officer, and a friendly one at that – because he wandered over to assist the stranded gang.

As he leaned in to the front window to offer his help, he spotted the tools, masks, and jewels.

At Snaresbrook Crown Court, Alasow pleaded not guilty and told the jury that he was in the area looking to buy the Rover – but he did it *in rhyme*.

They weren't impressed.

Unfortunately, I can't find a record of what he actually said, but here's my advice:

> Defendants really shouldn't speak in rap
> The jury will know you're talking crap.
> But if you insist on talking in rhyme
> You will end up doing time.

*

IF IT IS ANY CONSOLATION to the unfortunate Alasow – and I hope it isn't – he's not alone in forgetting to fill up a getaway car.

Danny Stewart sped away, doubtless whooping and cackling, in his Renault Clio with three accomplices, after netting £6,000 in a house raid.

But he'd hardly made it to the end of the road before the engine died. The 19-year-old numpty grabbed a jerry can and raced to the nearest petrol station, near Southend in Essex. The delay gave officers plenty of time to catch their man, a suspicious neighbour having dialled 999 after seeing the four men load up the Clio.

After the teenager was found guilty of burglary, a police spokesman said, 'This case was certainly made a lot easier thanks to our friend's unexpected pit stop.'

Stewart, a car valeter, denied being involved in the raid but was found guilty at Southend Crown Court. The prosecution case was helped by the fact that the cashier at the petrol station recognised Stewart, who was a regular customer, and thought it strange that he was so out of breath.

Jurors heard that, in an especially nasty twist, the gang had taken knives from the kitchen and left them strewn about the house, including one that was left embedded in the duvet. Sadly, the other gang members were not caught.

*

AT LEAST BUILDING society robber Richard Angel's vehicle had petrol in it. It also had a battery.

But the battery was flat.

Perhaps, as he turned the ignition key in vain, the 41-year-old considered the wisdom of buying a 12-year-old Ford Scorpio for £180 on eBay to use as a getaway car.

Up until that moment, it had all been going so well. Angel had patiently waited for three hours in the car outside a branch of the

Nationwide in Bournemouth. Of course, during that time the bozo had been listening to the radio, playing with the windows and generally running down the electrics.

When a cash delivery van pulled up, he jumped out in his hoodie and balaclava and pointed an imitation pistol bought for £99 at the terrified security guard, who handed over a cash box containing £18,000.

Subtracting his investments of £180 and £99, and bit more for the balaclava and hoodie, at that point the toerag was around £17,700 up on the deal.

He might have stayed that way if only the Scorpio had started.

When it failed to do so, Angel used a newspaper to try to set fire to it so as to destroy any incriminating evidence.

In that, too, he was a failure, and the police later found his fingerprints on en empty pop bottle.

He attempted to escape on foot, dumping the cash box, but chose a route that took him past a police station and was arrested virtually on the steps.

For the defence, Robert Gray told Bournemouth Crown Court, 'The planning here was amateurish. Would a professional, hardened, ruthless criminal buy a cheap car for £180 which isn't a reliable getaway vehicle? He didn't even start the car before getting out to commit the robbery to see if it still worked.'

The numbskull was jailed for six years.

*

AT FIRST SIGHT, bank robber James Snell, 27, seems to have been no fool.

He used a BMW in good nick for the job in hand, and it even had petrol in the tank *and* a fully-charged battery.

Trouble is, *it was his own car* – and it had a very distinctive personalised number plate, 'J4MES'.

He and two mates stole more than £100,000 in a 2009 midnight raid on a branch of the Halifax in Cardiff. The gang struck as security guards delivered cash, two of them smashing their way in with heavy drain covers they had pinched from the road nearby, and a third waving a baseball bat and shouting threats. So far, so good.

Unfortunately, a passer-by had earlier noticed the car – and its unusual registration plate – when it stopped for one of the men to steal a drain cover. 'It was the distinctiveness of the car which contributed to the robbers' undoing,' prosecutor Daniel Williams was later to tell Cardiff Crown Court.

Before sending them down for between eight and 12 years, Judge Gareth Jones called the operation 'professional' and 'sophisticated' – apart, that is, from driving a car with your name written on it.

*

THE ABOVE CASE reminds me of the story of an unusually arrogant armed robber called Patrick Maguire who had the number plate 'N10KED'. With a little tinkering, using a yellow screw to hide part of the '0', it read 'NICKED' – the idea being that this would wind up the cops.

It did.

Officers responded by placing a listening device in the car, which allowed them to overhear the fool and his accomplices planning to rob a post office in Gloucester. After Maguire was given an indeterminate jail sentence at Bristol Crown Court in 2007, an Inspector commented, 'I think the number plate was designed to taunt the police and impress his friends, but it now seems somewhat ironic, given the sentence imposed.'

*

NOT ALL ROBBERS use their own vehicles. Some prefer a taxi. David Field and an accomplice called a cab before going to a Holyhead branch of Argos, where they tried to leg it with two stolen widescreen televisions, jumping into the back seat, yelling at the cabbie 'Drive!'

Driver Darren Renton said, 'Are you having a laugh?'

Which was a particularly brave thing to do, because the pair had just been joined by two more accomplices.

But if Darren was calling their bluff, it was a good call. 'They really started to panic then,' he later told the local *Daily Post*, 'and started offering to make it worth my while, to pay me off. But I just told them to get out of the car. My wife said afterwards, "What if you'd been stabbed?" But I didn't think of that. I just wanted them out of the car. Looking back, I think it's really funny.'

Argos staff collected the televisions from the taxi while the gang escaped on foot. Field, 18, was caught and given a 12-month conditional discharge.

*

KEVIN FORRESTER ALSO used a taxi as his getaway vehicle after nicking a load of audio and recording equipment. But he was caught after the cops discovered he had *booked the taxi in his own name and had been dropped off at his own house.*

This astonishingly stupid episode occurred in Haverhill, Suffolk, in January 2012, after 33-year Forrester enlisted the help of a 28-year-old mate, Robert Scullion, to steal the audio equipment, worth around £7,500, from an outbuilding behind a house in the town.

The driver of the taxi, a large people-carrier, was suspicious of the haul and alerted police. Meanwhile, the owner of the recording equipment reported it stolen. As if that wasn't enough, neighbours where the burglary took place and more neighbours where Forrester lived also rang the police when the stolen goods were loaded and unloaded. In fact, in total, the police received 15 tip-offs. 'We couldn't really fail with this one,' said Inspector Peter Ferrie.

Forrester got 18 weeks' jail; Scullion received an 18-month community order and was told to attend something which I didn't know existed called a 'thinking skills programme'.

*

ANTHONY THACKER AT least used a fake name – 'Mr Smith', originally enough – when he booked a taxi after nicking a flatscreen television, DVD player and gold watch from a flat in Southsea, Portsmouth.

By way of payment, he offered the driver the watch and DVD player, which, for some reason, aroused the cabbie's suspicions.

It was a basic error for someone who already had 28 convictions for 62 offences. The offer was declined, but Thacker left the items in the car anyway. The driver called the police and Thacker was arrested.

'He was drunk at the time,' Portsmouth Crown Court heard in May 2012, prompting the response from Recorder David Bartlett, 'People don't want drunk burglars clambering into their houses or flats.'

Thacker got 12 months, suspended for two years.

*

NOW, CAR KEYS. So important when it comes to getting that car started, as bank robber David Carpenter would surely be the first to admit. He'd entered the Beneficial Savings Bank in Tabernacle Township, New Jersey, in December 2010 wearing a black sweatshirt and ski mask, and armed with a steak knife.

Vaulting the counter, he held the knife to the throat of one bank employee and demanded money.

Another employee handed over a plastic bag of notes, and Carpenter then made his getaway.

At which point, as so often, it all went pear-shaped.

He reached his Honda Civic parked nearby, but realised he'd dropped the keys inside the bank. So he raced back to the building, only to discover that staff had locked the doors behind him.

He escaped into a wooded area, but was arrested soon afterwards when a resident called 911 to report a man knocking on her door claiming he was looking for his lost dog and asking to use her phone.

*

WHICH BRINGS US to two hopeless Aussie car thieves. It's the first tale I've really struggled to get more detail on, and I dearly hope it's not an online myth. Here is the story in full as reported on many websites:

> TWO MEN have been arrested for allegedly trying to steal cars at Old Noarlunga. Adelaide police were called to Honeypot Road just after 1am after someone reported hearing noises near their family car. Police allege they found a man, 28, hiding in bushes and another, 53, locked inside the car he was trying to steal. Both are to appear in Christies Beach Magistrates Court today.

How dumb do you have to be get stuck inside the car you're pinching?

*

THIS IS A SIMILAR story that I *was* able to source. It concerns another Aussie thief – this time, one who fell asleep in a black Audi convertible.

He drove it into a car wash in Para Hills West, Adelaide, at about three in the morning and, when the car did not move for an hour, the attendant called police. They found the car had two different number plates and had been reported stolen from the city a week earlier. A 39-year-old was charged with illegal use of a motor vehicle and theft. It's just a wild guess, but I suspect drink or drugs may have been taken.

*

OF COURSE, THAT can happen to anyone. Ask burglar James Rollinson.

Rollinson spotted Diane Goodyear in a wine bar, and drew the correct, and cold-blooded, conclusion that her house was empty and ripe for raiding.

Part one of his plan went perfectly: he smashed a window, got in and grabbed Diane's car keys, jewellery, a games console, a laptop and a camera before fleeing in her car.

Part two wasn't so good.

The greedy git returned for more – but by now the effect of his own evening's drinking was kicking in.

He fell asleep in the car outside Diane's house.

A neighbour who spotted the smashed window in the house in Sedgley, West Midlands, alerted the police and 20-year-old Rollinson was arrested where he lay.

All the stolen goods apart from the camera were found back at his house. In April 2013 he was jailed for a year by Wolverhampton Crown Court.

His lawyer told the court that at the time Rollinson was 'tanked-up' and 'not in a sober, sensible and rational state of mind.'

I've never understood how that counts as mitigation, unless we as a country have decided that sober criminals deserve more serious sentences than drunk ones.

*

I DON'T THINK the following needs much elaboration (it was reported around the world, this version being from the *Austrian Times* in December 2011):

> A WOULD-BE car thief was arrested when he asked an off-duty policeman if he could help him hot-wire a Nissan hatchback he'd just broken into in Wroclaw, Poland.
>
> Officer Szymon Jadry told the crook to wait while he got some tools. Then he walked round the corner back to his police station, put his uniform back on, and returned to arrest him.

*

IN THIS AGE OF ID theft, you'd have thought that everyone realised the importance of shredding important financial documents – such as, say, the paperwork you've been using to carry out a long-term fraud.

Edmund Jaques was a dentist, and part of his practice involved visiting care homes to treat the elderly patients who lived there, and who couldn't travel to him.

Then he'd bill the NHS for all the cavities he'd filled.

But it turned out that some of the people he was claiming to have treated were actually filling cavities of their own – six feet under.

Jaques' *modus operandi* was to pinch lists of care home residents during his legitimate visits, and then use those details to file hundreds of false claims, faking patients' signatures.

Unfortunately, as Ipswich Crown Court heard, 'the population of care homes changes quite regularly' – the best euphemism I've ever heard for old folks popping their clogs – and, eventually, someone somewhere spotted that Jaques, 64, was 'treating' folks who had died.

By this time, he had swindled £78,000 out of the health service, having submitted 1,700 bogus claims.

When he came to court in March 2013, Jaques at first pleaded not guilty to fraud. But he later changed his mind – which was probably sensible, given that when the police raided his home they found one incredibly damning piece of evidence... the sheets of paper the crook had used to practice his fake signatures.

Where's a shredder when you need one?

He got 18 months inside.

*

I URGE YOU TO Google this one, because the picture of John Pearce hanging upside down inside the home he was trying to burgle is a joy.

Paul Ives was returning to his terraced house in Dartford, Kent, when he saw Pearce dangling inside his ground floor bay window, one foot caught on a shoelace at the top of the frame where he had smashed through the glass. The more he struggled, the more trapped he became.

Despite still having a hammer in his hand, Pearce denied trying to rob the house, insisting he had actually been trying to stop some other burglars.

By the time Mr Ives showed up, a small crowd of onlookers had gathered and they soon began to mock the hapless thief and take pictures.

One shot shows his exposed torso as his shirt and jacket hang down over his head, his track suit bottoms having gone in the other direction to expose his boxer shorts. One foot in a black trainer is outside the smashed glass, the other inside and firmly caught. 'He was screaming at us to get him down and we were all saying, "I don't think so",' Mr Ives told reporters.

A neighbour said, 'He was screaming in agony and swearing and shouting, "I'm not the burglar!" but I said, "Well, you are, aren't you?" One man walked past and said, "Hang in there, mate." It was all quite funny.'

Police and paramedics eventually arrived to free Pearce, and he was led away in handcuffs. He later changed his story and admitted burglary with intent to steal, and asked for 12 similar offences to be taken into consideration, to add to his tally of 50 more break-ins. He was jailed for three years in October 2008, Judge Jeremy Carey at Maidstone Crown Court remarking, 'This was an entry, albeit an incompetent and pathetic one which left him dangling from the window for more than an hour.'

*

THERE'S ANOTHER EXAMPLE of something similar from late 2010. This story is also worth an online search, because it comes with the lovely sight of the would-be burglar's bum and legs dangling outside a window in grey tracksuit bottoms, his naked torso and head stuck inside. Paul Keenan, 36, had tried squeezing in through the tiny bathroom window of a house in Bow, east London, at around two in the morning, and that's how the occupants found him when they got up at around 8.30am – his arms, shoulders and a shaven head sticking through into their white-tiled bathroom. Two fire engines and 10 fire-fighters had to use a ladder and bolt cutters to free the idiot. He didn't suffer any serious injury – except to his pride because, as in the case of John Pearce, a little crowd had gathered to enjoy his misery.

The prolific offender was later given four years' jail, Judge Timothy King telling him at Snaresbrook Crown Court: 'The sentences you have received have been increasing and more of your time has been spent behind bars than in freedom. I have little optimism that you will change.'

Apparently, while awaiting his court hearing, Keenan suffered some piss-taking at the hands of other inmates. Possibly in a bid to drum up some sympathy, Nicholas Cooper, defending, said, 'He is incredibly sorry for what he has done. Whilst on remand he has been singled out to be picked on because of the way he has been vilified in the papers, and this is something he feels very keenly.'

Nope, I still don't feel sorry for him.

*

BURGLAR DAVID DUNIGAN also added to the gaiety of the nation by getting stuck half in and half out of a house. He used his pretend job as a window cleaner to size-up houses in Colchester, Essex, and would break-in if no one was at home

But clearly he didn't do his research well enough, because the 25-year-old found himself trapped when he tried to squeeze through a small bathroom window.

A passer-by saw his legs flapping in the breeze, and called Essex Police. The cops in that neck of the woods had been searching for the crook for some time – he had been on their Most Wanted list for two years – and officers could hardly believe their luck when they turned up at the scene.

In November 2012 he was jailed for two years after admitting four burglaries and asking for a further three attempted burglaries to be taken into consideration.

The house where he had got stuck belonged to Karen Riley, who was at work at the time. She later said, 'The window is very small… you couldn't fit through it unless you were a child or had a really tiny head.'

Well, Dunigan does appear to have a really tiny brain. Maybe he drew the wrong conclusion about the size of his head?

*

BESIDES LEAVING SOME spectacular evidence for the police, George Fairclough deserves a place here for his unusually horrible act of cowardicc.

The 21-year-old broke into the home of 84-year-old Richard Brough, and waited for the pensioner to return from an evening out.

What followed was a short and nasty struggle, with the young Fairclough inevitably over-powering a man more than 60 years his senior. The photograph of poor Richard's bruised and bloodied face, carried by the *Liverpool Post* in September 2012, would turn any stomach.

After the fight, he was tied up in his living room and gagged with a tea towel. Fairclough, who hid behind a balaclava and put on a fake accent, demanded the PIN for Richard's ATM card. Then he left, tried to withdraw some cash, discovered that he'd been duped and returned to Richard's house. 'You've given me the wrong f***ing number,' he shouted, as Liverpool Crown Court was later told. 'If you give me the right number, I'll come back and let you go. If you give me the wrong number I will come back and f***ing kill you.'

Understandably, Richard then revealed the correct number. Fairclough called a taxi and left, taking the elderly man's plasma screen television with him. *En route* home to Southport, he stopped to take £550 from Richard's account.

Meanwhile, the pensioner, thankfully, had struggled free, got outside and flagged down a passing car. The police responded quickly, and quickly found a clue left by the thuggish idiot.

Fairclough had made one spectacular blunder. When not making money by robbing defenceless old men, he carried out odd-jobs, touting for work by distributing flyers. Richard had been one of his customers, Fairclough having done some gardening for him. Police found one of Fairclough's flyers in Richard's house, and on it was a mobile phone number.

And what do you know? It was the same number that Fairclough had used to call his getaway taxi.

In October 2012, a judge at Liverpool Crown Court sentenced him to ten years in prison.

In contrast to the actions of that waste of skin, here's what the magnificent Richard Brough had to say at the end of the case: 'I have no hard feelings. I'm just glad the whole thing is over. I have no animosity or any feelings one way or the other, except that he's better off where he is.'

*

DIDN'T KEVIN COSTNER make a film about this? *Prints of Thieves* I think it was called?

Anyway, from the *Dewsbury Reporter* in West Yorkshire comes the tale of two brothers who ran home after three break-ins, leaving a trail of footprints in the snow that led police straight to their front doors.

Outside one house was a pair of wet trainers which matched the footprints, and inside officers found Michael Coulson sitting at the bottom of the stairs texting.

Police followed the second set of footprints to another house, and found Dale Coulson hiding in the loft.

In April 2013, both brothers admitted three counts of attempted burglary. Michael Coulson got two years in a young offender institution, suspended for 12 months, plus 200 hours unpaid work. Dale, described by the judge as having 'an appalling record' that included theft, assault, witness intimidation and robbery, got three years. According to his lawyer he wants to join the Foreign Legion.

So, fingers crossed, he's leaving the country when he gets out of jail.

*

THE SNOW ALSO lay deep and crisp and even on the streets of Crossmichael, Kirkcudbrightshire at Christmas time, and drugged-up burglar Thomas Branney was full of the festive spirit – plus a handful of valium tablets.

So much so that he decided he'd wrap up warm and go out for a spot of late-night house-breaking. He got into the house of an 80-year-old grandmother – terrifying her when she woke up to find him looming over her bed – and escaped with £250-worth of Christmas presents for her grandchildren, and other valuables.

So far, so good – for Branney, that is, who thought he'd got clean away with his haul.

Unfortunately, the dummy had forgotten what happens when you walk through snow. The police simply followed the trail of footprints which led back to his home and nicked him. The 44-year-old was jailed for 13 months at Kirkcudbright Sheriff's Court.

*

ACTUALLY SNOW SEEMS to be a real problem for your dimmer Scots crim. John Honeyman broke into a shed in Bathgate, West Lothian, in December 2011, and stole two mini-motorbikes worth £600. Wind forward to the hearing two months later at Livingstone Sheriff Court, and John Barclay, prosecuting, is explaining how the householder tracked down the 20-year-old thief.

'Because of the snow which had fallen overnight,' he said, 'she was able to follow footprints all the way to the accused's house. She didn't enter but contacted the police.'

In defence, the court heard that Honeyman had gone to take back a mini-motorbike that had been stolen from him but went on to take two others as well.

So, how would Sheriff David Hall describe Honeyman's actions? 'Botched'.

He was fined £300.

*

MONTANA. ANOTHER PLACE where you'd expect criminals to be used to the hazards caused by snow – unless they have the fantastically appropriate surname of 'Klotz'.

In November 2011, *The Great Falls Tribune* reported how Casey Ann Klotz, 24, had been arrested after shoplifting clothes worth around £100 from a department store. A security guard had challenged her but was pushed against a glass door by her companion, the equally superbly-named John Heavyrunner, 18. Police were called and – guess what? – followed their footsteps through the snow to their trailer home.

*

SO, WHAT WAS THE evidence that helped jail prolific car thieves David Leadbetter and Sam Holmes?

Well, there were the fingerprints.

Oh, and some DNA helped too.

Plus number plate recognition data, that helped a lot.

As did details of their movements stored in the SatNav.

And then there were those pictures that the two of them took of themselves behind the wheels of the stolen motors.

During their spree, from May to July 2012, the pair stole 35 high-performance cars to order from London, Kent, Surrey and Hampshire, taking vehicles worth almost £500,000.

Other gang members would break in to their target houses, take the keys, and the pair would then drive off into the night, in one instance forcing a woman who stood in front of her car to jump aside or face being mown down.

In April 2013, Maidstone Crown Court heard how Holmes, 22,

enjoyed 'the feeling of being in control', which was ironic considering that they left so much evidence for the police that the inevitable result would be that they'd end up in jail and with no control at all over their lives.

Along with 23-year-old Leadbeater, Holmes originally pleaded not guilty to conspiracy to commit burglary. The trial had got underway and was set to last up to six weeks, but after just one day of hearing the prosecution case the pair threw in the towel and changed their pleas to guilty. They were jailed for six years.

'Incompetent' and 'without morals' is how they were described by Detective Constable Adrian Grew of Kent and Essex Serious Crime Directorate. 'They may have seen themselves as successful criminals,' he said, 'but they left an incredible trail of evidence and slipped up in every way possible.'

*

OH, THE HAZARDS of being a teenage burglar/member of the Facebook Generation. There you are, in your victim's house with a couple of her diamond rings worth hundreds of pounds in your pocket and a computer sitting temptingly on a nearby table. What to do? Scarper with just the expensive rings? Or take the computer as well? Or – just maybe – log on to the computer to update your Facebook status?

Jonathan G Parker, of Fort Loudoun, Pennsylvania, chose a strange combination of options 1 and 3. According to the Berkeley County Sheriff's Department, the homeowner got back to find a bedroom window broken, cabinets pulled open and two rings worth around £2,000 missing – but her computer was still there, it was still switched on and it was still open on Parker's Facebook page. Better still, a friend of the victim recognised Parker and knew where he lived. He was arrested within hours.

*

PARKER IS NOT unique in his unhelpful Facebook obsession. Indeed, it seems to be an international phenomenon. This, from the *Argentina Independent* of 4 October, 2011:

> A 17-YEAR-OLD trying to rob a shop was caught for being distracted by his Facebook page. The teenager broke his way into a sporting goods store on Calle 7 and 58 yesterday, in the city of La Plata. He tried on shirts and stuffed objects in his pocket, before spotting a computer. He proceeded to browse the internet and check his Facebook account, giving time for the officers from the comisaría nueve [the local police station] who had been alerted, to find and arrest him.

*

BACK HOME IN the West Midlands, Lenny Loveridge, 19, visited an elderly gent that he knew in Brierley Hill near Stourbridge with a pal. The pair distracted the man and stole his television (which they later sold for £25). But detectives were on to them quickly. Before pinching the TV, Loveridge had asked to use his victim's computer to check – you've guessed it – his messages on Facebook.

He was later jailed for a year at Wolverhampton Crown Court, and was told by Recorder David Herbert, 'This was on any view a mean offence against a vulnerable victim.'

Loveridge's lawyer described it as a 'curious' burglary.

'It was inevitable that he would be caught,' said the barrister. 'This was a very poorly thought-out offence and the pair were always going to end up in court.'

*

DEBASISH MAJUMDER ALSO got caught thanks to his computer habits, though in his case it did not involve any analysis of his Facebook page. It just needed someone to watch what he was looking at – and that someone was a judge.

Majumder was a 54-year-old clerk at Inner London Crown Court. During a rape trial, where he found the evidence a touch tedious, he whiled away the time by watching explicit online porn – literally right under the nose of Judge Nigel Seed QC, who was sitting behind him on the bench.

When questioned, Majumder, who had worked for the court service for 27 years, admitted routinely watching internet porn when he was bored. He was jailed for seven months, suspended for two years.

Judge Nicholas Price QC said, 'I'm told by your counsel that you didn't think anyone could see what you were doing. You were wrong. The very fact there are no comparable cases shows how rare, if not unique, your case must be.'

*

ELIDON HABILAJ, a 35-year-old illegal immigrant from Albania, lied to get a British passport and used a false name and backstory (he claimed he was a refugee from Kosovo) to wangle a job with the Serious Organised Crime Agency.

(Perhaps this tells us something about the Serious Organised Crime Agency?)

While working at SOCA, he couldn't resist searching for his own real details on an international database… and when he double-clicked on his name, his photo appeared.

Unfortunately, his boss was walking past at the time.

Habilaj got 18 months in prison at Snaresbrook Crown Court in January 2013, but skipped bail and fled to Albania.

Some people might have preferred 18 months in Pentonville.

*

SICILIAN DRUG DEALER Michele Grasso fled from his home town of Taormina in 2010 to escape the law.

At first, he did a reasonable job of hiding, mocking officers by posting on his Facebook page that his new address was 'Alcatraz'.

But later that year he started to give away a few actual clues, starting with pictures of himself building a snowman and asking 'Have you seen how beautiful it is here with the snow?'

A friend then posted on his Wall, 'Why don't you let me know where you are? Is it in case you get caught?'

Grasso responded with even more specific clues. Under the title 'Christmas in London', he posted shots of visits to landmarks including the London Eye and Tower Bridge. Next came a picture of himself with an arm around a woman and the title, 'My 24th birthday (in London)'.

The following year, a court in Sicily sentenced Grasso *in absentia* to five years in prison. But the irrepressible idiot just carried on giving away info as to his whereabouts. By January 2012, more cocky – or more dumb – than ever, he posted shots of himself working in the kitchen of a pizzeria in Woodford Green, north London, and even added external pictures showing the restaurant's name. He also shared pics of himself at Madame Tussauds posing with waxworks of Barack Obama, Tom Cruise and David Beckham.

The Italian police contacted their counterparts in Britain and the following month Grasso was arrested and extradited.

The *Daily Telegraph* version of the story reminded readers of a similar case, when a woman had inadvertently betrayed her fugitive mafia boyfriend by uploading their holiday snaps onto Facebook. Police had thought that Salvatore D'Avino, who'd been on the run for four years and was on the list of Italy's 100 most-wanted criminals, was hiding out under a false identity in the Moroccan hills. But thanks to those Facebook pictures, the rather more mundane truth was revealed, and he was arrested as he was filling up at a petrol station near Marbella on the Costa del Sol.

*

'BIG FAT GYPSY SWINDLERS' is how the *Daily Star* put it, with typical delicacy.

The paper had in mind a gang which ran a cowboy building racket, and which was ordered in March 2012 to repay £1.3 million to its victims.

Frank Tomney, 55, his twin sons and a nephew tricked 42 householders into paying extortionate fees for botched jobs.

The Tomneys lived on a caravan site in Cleveleys, Lancs, and during raids on their homes the police found three secure boxes with cash inside totalling £480,775.

In November 2011, Tomney was jailed for five-and-a-half years for conspiracy to commit fraud and tax evasion. His 21-year-old twin sons Frank jnr and Thomas were sent down for five years and four-and-a-half years respectively for conspiracy to commit fraud, and nephew Brian Tomney, 29, of Salford, was jailed for four-and-a-half years for tax evasion and fraud.

Which is all well and good, but what concerns us here is how were they caught.

Answer: Frank Jnr put a film of himself on YouTube bragging how he used a 98p carton of milk as driveway sealant to con an ex-serviceman out of £800.

*

I POSTED THE following on the *Daily Mirror*'s website in October 2010:

> A BUNGLING couple convicted of selling almost 600 pirated CDs at a market tried to claim the discs were not theirs. And it might just have worked, apart from one tiny detail…
>
> Husband and wife Dennis Davis, 40, and 34-year-old Kerry Ann Graham, of South Norwood, London – who were also caught selling fake Nike trainers – were nabbed by Surrey County Council trading standards,

from which office one Lucy Corrie said, 'This couple aren't quite Bonnie and Clyde, and it probably wasn't the smartest move by Dennis to put his own photograph on the illegal items he was selling.'

*

IN 2011, THE SCALE of the problems caused by metal thieves became important news – and a major political topic.

Mainly, the culprits strike late at night. The railways are often targeted for their copper cabling; the lead on church roofs is also popular in the criminal fraternity (that year was the worst on record, with more than 2,500 claims being made to the main Church of England insurer). So it is of some comfort to know that not all of these scrotes escape justice.

Saulius Ciuzas stripped £10,000-worth of lead from the roof of a 12th century church in Boston, Lincs, but when he fled the Lithuanian thief left behind a vital clue – a can of lager. Not just any lager, but an Eastern European brand, Lech, which had his DNA on it.

Ciuzas denied any involvement in the lead theft. He admitted drinking Lech every day, but he had no explanation for how a can of the lager containing his DNA came to be on the roof of the St Peter and St Paul Church.

The 39-year-old was jailed for 12 months.

The website *thisislincolnshire* quoted Reverend Gary Morgan saying, 'We are pleased justice has been done, and hope he learns from his experience. On this occasion, over £10,000 of lead was stripped from the roof, but there had been two previous lead thefts which is very dispiriting. Hopefully, the fact that somebody has been caught will dissuade others, but it makes it impossible to leave our churches open – if they were they would be stripped bare.'

*

IS IT STUPIDITY, or is it laziness? Of all the shops, petrol stations, bookies and banks in the country, some criminals just have to go and rob their local one – the one where there's the best chance they'll be recognised.

As Anthony Gorman discovered.

He was known far and wide as 'Spider' – even by the shopkeeper he tried to rob.

And what a robbery it was.

The 21-year-old walked into the general store in Longsight, Manchester, disguised with a dark cap, balaclava and his coat collar pulled high over his face, pointed an imitation handgun at shopkeeper Michael Singh, and yelled, 'Put the f***ing money in the bag or I'll shoot you!'

He'd picked the wrong target. Michael, who had been meditating only moments earlier, refused to open the till, shouting back, 'Are you stupid? No, you can't have it! Get out!'

A tussle followed, Manchester Crown Court later heard, in which Mr Singh managed to divest the gormless Gorman of his fake gun, balaclava, and even the coat, which meant that when the idiot fled he was one of the few robbers in history to leave the target shop with less than he had come in with.

Perhaps Gorman was embarrassed by this ignominious fact. It's certainly hard to think of any other rational explanation for what happened next: he returned to the store *and asked for his coat back*.

According to Mr Singh, he was even quite polite about it. He said 'please'.

'I just cannot believe anyone could be so stupid as to ask for his coat back after bungling a robbery,' said the shopkeeper. 'He should have just cut his losses and run.'

In sentencing Gorman to four-and-a-half years, Judge Martin Steiger QC remarked, with considerable understatement, 'This was hardly a professionally-executed offence.'

*

ASBESTOS IS WELL-KNOWN to have a devastating effect on the lungs. Perhaps it mangles the brain, as well, if the disastrous robbery carried out by Neil Simons is anything to go on.

The 27-year-old had been doing very nicely, and legally, earning £1,000 a week as an asbestos remover until he decided on a career change – a move into armed robbery.

First, he bought himself a disguise – in the shape of a Halloween zombie mask. Then, three days later, he walked into a petrol station around the corner from his home in Cardiff wearing the mask and a high visibility jacket, produced an axe and demanded cash. He got away with around £50, but he had over-looked one crucial factor. He had bought the £3.99 mask *from the same petrol station* shortly before, and – obviously – hadn't been in disguise at the time.

What's more, no-one else had bought that particular mask, so it was an easy enough job to trawl through the old CCTV footage and dig out his picture.

Simons, who was also convicted of attempting to rob a nearby newsagent's and a post office, got a five-year stretch. But the sobering fact is, he may well still be at large if he could have been bothered to buy the mask from a different petrol station.

*

COCAINE AND BOOZE left Alan Ford so addled that he returned to the shop he had robbed the previous day to buy an ice lolly.

The jobless 37-year-old had been on a drink and drugs binge after being dumped by his girlfriend – it's hard to imagine why, he sounds like a real catch – when he went to an Indian takeaway in Kirkcaldy, Fife. He jumped over the counter and, brandishing a knife, ordered the assistant, 32-year-old Ruqya Bano, to open the till, yelling 'Don't come near me!'

He fled with £160. Four young women who were waiting in a car outside and who witnessed the robbery tried following but lost him, and he would probably have got away scot free (an initial police

search came up blank) had he not decided to go to the shop that's attached to the takeaway the following day for the lolly.

Ruqya recognised him, called the police and then tailed the toerag in her car until CID officers intercepted him.

*

ROBBER Brian Decktor was caught red-handed – and purple-handed – when he robbed a security van with two accomplices.

They got away with a cash box containing £25,000 and hotfooted it back to Brian's pad in Dagenham, Essex, to share out the loot.

But they were complete amateurs, and didn't know that these boxes contain a clever little security feature. When the gleeful felons chiselled their way into the box, they triggered a cartridge filled with dye which exploded, turning 22-year-old Decktor's hands, and the cash, purple.

Then there was a knock on the door. Decktor, clutching wads of purple banknotes, opened it to find the police.

'Two more bundles of dye-stained cash were found in his lounge,' prosecutor Katherine Lumsdon told the local crown court in February 2011. Decktor got six months in jail.

*

'LUDICROUSLY INCOMPETENT' – that was the official verdict from Judge Jeremy Gold on baby-faced robber Sam Brown, who had held-up staff in a bookies at knifepoint and made off with £360. Less than three hours earlier, the 23-year-old been in the same bookies busy losing money – and had shown them his driving licence to prove his age.

It was December 23, 2010, when Brown first went into the branch of Coral's in Sittingbourne, Kent. After wasting money on a bet and gaming machines, he left, changed his clothes, and returned, just as the bookies had closed. A female member of staff, recognising him from the earlier visit, let him in, perhaps assuming he had left something behind. Once Brown was inside with the woman, he produced a knife and threatened her. After escaping with the cash, he went to buy to some booze to drink with mates. In mitigation, Maidstone Crown Court heard that Brown, who had previous convictions for robbery and burglary, was drunk and stoned at the time. You don't say.

He was also said to be depressed at the thought of spending Christmas alone after falling out with his family. He got five Christmases inside (though will be out after two).

*

DAVID FLETCHER HAD lived at his house in Winsford, Cheshire, for six years without mishap. Then one day, a neighbour, Michael Hill, visited him for the first time – and the very next day Mr Fletcher was burgled.

Hmmm. Could this be a coincidence?

The missing items included a 50-inch plasma television, a laptop and charger, a games console, a DVD player, and fishing equipment. Police searched Hill's house, five doors away, and found Mr Fletcher's games console. The laptop was found in Hill's car, the television was at a different address, and the fishing gear had already been sold to a cash converter shop.

Hill, a 'heavy sporadic drug user', got 12 months' jail.

*

JAMIE ALEXANDER didn't even bother walking five doors down to find a victim – he picked on the poor bloke next door, Jason Rendall. The 18-year-old simpleton was caught when Jason looked through Alexander's window and saw the crook wearing his distinctive, striped jumper and puzzling over how to get his stolen flat-screen television to work.

Jason had come back from work to find that a living room window had been smashed at his home in St Ninians, Stirling. The back door was open, and a number of things were missing, including the 42-inch telly, a Sky HD and Freeview box, CDs, DVDs and children's toys.

'I went in to the garden, looked at my neighbour's house and there he was – wearing my jumper and trying to tune in my TV,' he said. 'He was wearing my jeans as well. I was fizzing mad, but even I had to laugh at his stupidity.'

The thief had even had the cheek to use one of Mr Rendall's own hammers, stolen from his shed, to smash the window.

Stirling Sheriff Court heard that Alexander was trying to deal with a drugs problem. Of course he was. He got seven months' jail.

The verdict from the *Daily Record* was, 'Scotland's thickest robber'.

*

NATHAN KENNEDY ALSO ransacked his immediate neighbour, but was at least a little more subtle about it.

His victim, Neil Barton, was baffled when he was burgled twice in one week, despite all of his doors remaining locked. A friend suggested that Neil check his loft – where he found that a hole had been knocked through the adjoining wall, and a crude attempt made to cover it with some loose bricks and cardboard. He peered through the hole and saw some of his stolen property in Kennedy's attic.

Then it all made sense. Mr Barton had heard the banging as Kennedy had made the hole, but had just assumed that it was some innocent DIY.

The thief, whose haul was worth £3,500, was sentenced to 42 months in jail at Bristol Crown Court.

The Sun, incidentally, ran this under the headline 'Next Door Nabber', and *The Daily Mail*'s website carries one interesting comment:

> 'Nothing new here. I am an ex-police officer and I often came across this. On one occasion, we climbed through next door and the burglar, who had simply gone back to his bed with the loot at his side, was sound asleep! Doh!'

*

STUPID THINGS TO DO with a disguise, No1: Take it off *during* the robbery.

David Reid cut two holes in a pillow case before going to a grocer in Perth with a screwdriver and demanding cash, cigarettes and a bottle of Buckfast (fortified wine, known as 'Buckie' by its admirers). But the pillow case slipped over his eyes, and Reid started bumping into the displays so he took it off. Since the 21-year-old was a regular customer, he was naturally recognised immediately. He quickly realised his error, and fled in panic and confusion with £90.

He was arrested within 10 minutes – still, for reasons I can only guess at, in possession of the pillow case disguise.

In mitigation a court was told – you can probably guess what's coming – that he was high on drink and drugs at the time.

*

RICHARD MILLARD ALSO made the mistake of robbing a shop where he was a regular customer, but you could argue that he was more successful than David Reid – he stayed at large for fully 12 minutes after the robbery before he was caught. Despite wearing a balaclava which left only his eyes visible, he was recognised instantly by shop assistant Sylvia Bailey. She'd worked in the store for 30 years, and knew everyone in the area.

'She did wonder why he was wearing the balaclava, but was not particularly concerned because she knew he was a little odd,' Warwick Crown Court was later told.

All became clear when Millard leaned over the counter and pulled out a knife. Sylvia and other customers left the store in Dordon, Staffordshire, and called the police, while the 29-year-old helped himself to £90 and some fags. When arrested at his home less than a quarter of an hour after the crime, Millard, a heroin addict (naturally), told police, 'I suppose you're here because of the robbery. I did it.'

He got three years and three months.

*

AARON BUTLER WAS called 'sick' by several papers, and they had a point. He was asked to identify the body of his 68-year-old neighbour in Barrow-in-Furness, Cumbria, who had died unexpectedly – though not in suspicious circumstances.

Later, after the corpse of Amy Backhouse was removed, and once the house was empty of police officers and relatives, he rang two mates and they raided it, getting away with the dead woman's flat-screen television and handbag.

Suspicious workmen dialled 999 after seeing the gang leaving the house with their faces covered, and the TV was found in the back garden of one of Butler's accomplices, 24-year-old Carr Metcalfe.

'This is one of the most despicable and heartless crimes I have investigated,' said Detective Constable Amy Loebell, of Cumbria Police. 'As her neighbour, Butler was the person who initially identified Mrs Backhouse's body and yet he chose to steal her TV less than one hour after her grieving family had left the area.'

Butler, 23, was jailed for 15 months.

*

COMBINE STUPID CRIMINALS with mobile phones, and you have a rich seam of bungling incompetence.

Sean Mooney was one of many dopey looters who spent the summer of 2011 trashing shops during the 'retail riots'.

Peter Brewerton was woken by a call at 2.30am to warn him that his picture framing shop in Bristol was under attack.

(Remember that these riots were allegedly sparked by the shooting of a gun-toting gangster in London, and ask yourself who would want to take out their 'anger' at this on a picture framer who lived 120 miles away. But I digress.)

When Mr Brewerton arrived, he found the front window had been smashed, pictures were strewn over the street, and the float had been stolen from the till.

And next to the till was a mobile phone.

Certain that it did not belong to any of his staff, Peter handed it to the police, who traced it to 29-year-old Mooney.

He claimed to have had nothing to do with the looting, saying that the phone had been pinched a week earlier, but that was a tough – and stupid – defence to run with, given that the phone contained text messages that he'd sent using his nickname on the night in question.

He was jailed for 32 months after admitting two counts of burglary – the other was a house break-in, which was another vignette of stupidity. Some of the items he took were of no financial value but caused enormous pain to the householder – among them were *locks of his children's hair and their milk teeth*. Why would *anyone* steal those?

Mooney also stole a laptop and computer game console. The occupant, something of a sleuth, talked to locals who ran second-hand and pawn shops, and one confirmed that a man had tried to sell him the stolen items (though sadly the personal items were never recovered). Better still, his picture was on CCTV. When police arrested Mooney, he denied being involved in the burglary, just as he denied looting the picture framing shop, but it was a denial that collapsed when his DNA was found on a smashed window at the house.

*

LONDON RIOTER ANDREW Burls, 23, ended up with a decent stretch for his part in an arson attack which saw a fire start in a boutique before gutting the adjacent Greggs bakery and a post office. The damage came to more than £1 mllion and six people were left homeless – so in many ways, it's not all that funny a story.

But how was he caught? A CCTV image does not at first seem promising, showing a face covered with a dark bandana and a baseball cap pulled down low over his forehead. Only the bridge of his nose and his eyes and ears are visible.

But what eyes they are!

Burls, you see, is cross-eyed. Massively.

The dummy had forgotten to cover them up with shades, and that proved his undoing. As Inner London Crown Court later heard from prosecutor Tom Forster, 'What's important about that image is that his eyes appear distinctive in that they appear to look in different directions.'

What he was actually looking at – albeit in a slighty skew-whiff fashion – was eight years in the jug.

*

HERE'S WHAT ONE detective chief inspector had to say about a prolific diamond robber: 'Torres played a central role in what were frightening and very well-executed robberies. His raids were organised, sophisticated and used a high level of violence to ensure that demands were met.'

Well-executed... organised... sophisticated... but also shot through with a lovely dose of stupid.

Jose-Jov Torres, a 32-year-old Mexican who lived in south London, was part of a gang which snatched gems worth £2.5million from businessmen in a five-month crime spree across Britain. Victims had their cars rammed and screwdrivers held to their throats in attacks that Blackfriars Crown Court was told were 'truly terrifying'.

Torres didn't help himself when he tossed aside a cigarette butt by his abandoned getaway car – the butt had his DNA on it. But dafter – and more incriminating – still was the Blackberry that was left at the scene of one attack. It was stolen and could not have been traced to Torres – were it not for the fact that the fool had only gone and taken pictures of himself on it.

That lovely piece of dim-wittedness led to him being jailed for 10 years, which can't have pleased him – but I suspect that what upset the arrogant thug the most is being branded 'a bungler' in the papers.

*

WHAT ELSE HAS been dropped at the scene of crime? Burglar Mark Cooper was tracked down and jailed after he left his Jobseeker's Allowance paperwork at the garage he had repeatedly targeted. The 23-year-old broke into West Exe Motors, in Tiverton, Devon, five times in two months, leaving the owner with a bill of more than £2,000 for repairs, the excess to pay on his insurance, plus the continual worry over when the next break-in would happen.

Mark Davies, 24, stole a van in Prestatyn, north Wales, and, after taking it for a spin, abandoned it. He left his bag in the van, reported *The Daily Post*, and he left a fixed penalty notice in the bag.

In December 2011, the Rhyl-based idiot was sentenced to a three month suspended prison sentence after admitting aggravated vehicle-taking, driving whilst disqualified, having no insurance and breaching a conditional discharge.

Mark Hunt broke into a house in Easington Colliery, County Durham, to get his hands on the Christmas presents inside. When he left the house, he was up by one television and one PlayStation, but unfortunately – for him – he was down by one mobile phone. Just to be sure of getting caught, he'd also left behind a shoe print that matched his trainers. In jailing the 28-year-old for two years and nine months, Judge Christopher Prince said that the offence was aggravated by being carried out only a month after he had been given a suspended sentence for affray.

*

WHAT I CAN'T UNDERSTAND is why anyone would take their mobile to a burglary in the first place?

Even if you don't accidentally drop it, there's a chance that it will be taken from you by force, as Mark Watson discovered.

The 'recovering' Scottish heroin addict caused damaged estimated at £370 when he smashed his way into a house in Galashiels, and was busy stuffing clothing, jewellery, a PlayStation and computer games into a holdall when William O'Docherty, the householder, returned. O'Docherty was not impressed and launched himself at Watson.

Reporting the subsequent court case in September 2011, *The Border Telegraph* noted, 'The accused managed to wriggle free and then went out of the house through the window he had broken but the householder had pulled the cap and body-warmer from him.'

And inside the body-warmer was Watson's keys and mobile – containing photographs of himself. With five previous convictions for housebreaking, he got eight months in jail.

*

IT'S DECEMBER 2012 and 24-year-old Stuart Gibbs is on trial for burglary at Leicester Crown Court.

He'd been found hiding in a shed behind the house he had targeted. The back door had been smashed causing damage put at £400, and glass on his gloves matched the glass from the broken window.

But that wasn't the best bit of evidence against him. It was a text that police found on his mobile (yes, he had it with him) which he'd sent two hours earlier to a mate who'd been pestering him:

> I've told you 20 times – don't ring me when I'm out robbing!

UR jailed 4 18 mnths LOL

*

MOBILES ARE A PROBLEM for thick thieves the world over. In India, a robber was caught by police after he returned to his victim's home and offered to swap stolen items for a phone he had accidentally left behind.

No wonder he wanted it back – being vain as well as stupid, the burglar had used a picture of himself as the screensaver. Ahmed Mubarak burst into the house of Pazha Karuppaiah, a state politician, before ripping an expensive gold chain from his wife's neck, *The Times of India* reported.

She called the police, but to her amazement, the first person to arrive at her home in Chennai, south-eastern India, was her assailant. He offered to return the gold chain in exchange for the mobile, but fled when officers arrived. He wasn't at large for long – even without the helpful screensaver, he was easily identified by the phone's address book.

Mubarak told the police it was his first attempt at robbery.

*

MOBILES SHOULD BE a godsend for your local have-a-go drug dealer. They make arranging a deal so much simpler. Except if you're Travis Huffman, from Texas. The shaven-headed 25-year-old no-hoper – the poor skinhead looks like he's about to burst into tears in his police mug shot – was jailed after he punched in the wrong the number when he was texting details of a drugs deal. The recipient of the accidental message? A police officer. Undercover cops played along and met Huffman, who was hoping to flog a stash of the painkiller hydrocodone.

'What Mr Huffman did today was kind of a self-service felony arrest,' said Kenneth Hayden of Montgomery County police with, I sense, something of a chuckle.

It gets better. Police raided Huffman's house and arrested his mother Kimberley 'Butterbean' Meadows, 43, for marijuana possession.

In an apparent attempt to take some of the heat off her son, she then courageously – or stupidly – claimed that the original drug deal had been for their mutual benefit. But, as a *Houston Press* blog reported, 'Sadly, Montgomery County cops are apparently immune to such kamikaze acts of parental chivalry. Instead of letting Huffman off the hook, they slapped Butterbean with the same state jail felony delivery of a controlled substance her son was already facing.'

Back to Kenneth Hayden of Montgomery's finest: 'We arrested Ms Meadows on a misdemeanour marijuana charge, and she talked her way into a felony charge.'

*

A BRIEF BUT dishonourable mention for Jason Topper. The 34-year-old was charged by police in Los Angeles with armed robbery after allegedly snatching a woman's handbag. He was caught after police searched for a man matching the description of the robber; when they spotted Topper they craftily dialled the victim's mobile, which had been in her handbag.

It rang in Topper's pocket.

*

MOBILES ARE A PARTICULAR hazard in the States, where it's easy to unwittingly hit the emergency speed-dial 911 button, especially if you've stuffed your phone into tight trouser pockets without the lock button on. In among all the annoying but innocent accidental calls to the police that this produces there are some criminal gems.

Ronald, Thomas and Allen Euson – never mind their exact relationship, suffice it to say they've got a lot of genetic material in common – were driving through Syracuse in New York State in April 2011 when one of them inadvertently butt-dialled (as it's delightfully known) the police, and a 911 dispatcher became privy to their conversation. Unfortunately for the Euson clan, this involved not only bragging about a recent robbery but discussing which businesses should be next on their hit list. Guided by descriptions in their conversation of the surrounding area, the police moved in, but they had no idea what sort of car they were looking for. Then, as one squad car passed a Kia Sportage, the dispatcher heard one of the three remark, 'There go the cops now!'

The squad car turned around and stopped the Kia. It was found to contain stolen property, and the hapless trio were charged with grand larceny, proving that smart phone does not equal smart caller.

*

STILL IN THE STATES, from Suffolk, Virginia, comes the little story of another burglar who went out of his way to make life easy for local police. He took a picture of himself flashing the gangsta hoodie horizontal v-sign on a phone he found lying around in a house he'd broken into... and then forgot to steal the phone. City police spokeswoman Debbie George said it was common for thieves to take pictures of themselves with their loot, but that they usually wait until they've actually stolen the stuff.

*

THE FOLLOWING GANG of home-grown no-hopers also pictured themselves with their loot. The pictures were taken on a mobile phone, which wasn't a problem... until the phone fell into police hands.

The teenage trio – one 17-year-old and two aged 16 – robbed a Texaco garage in Blackley, Manchester, in August 2011. It was around 5.20am and one of them pointed a firearm (or imitation firearm) at the sole member of staff on duty. They scarpered with £470 in cash and a load of cigarettes, and probably thought they'd made a clean getaway – hence the smug, gloating mobile phone picture of the loot piled on the lap of one of them sitting on a sofa.

But the police had quite a bit to go on. First, an officer had stopped the trio and questioned them as they loitered outside the garage earlier that morning. Unwisely, they still went ahead with the robbery, wearing hoodies to hide their faces. Their clothes, as pictured on CCTV, didn't quite match those of the three youths earlier questioned by the officer, a mystery that was quickly solved: they'd simply taken off their jackets and turned them inside out. Police raids followed.

'One had a rather large crow bar and we also found his clothes inside out, which isn't that unusual for a lad of that age, but when we seized it we did a comparison and forensics and it transpired that it all matched,' said Det Sgt Paul Copplestone of Greater Manchester Police. 'The pictures we found of one of them with the money was a nail in the coffin.'

The gang each got 14 months in a Young Offenders' Institution.

I suppose it is just stating the obvious to point out that the gang didn't care what harm they caused to the poor cashier, otherwise they would never had carried out the raid, but for the record, here's what he said in a victim impact statement: 'At the time, and still now, I think it was a gun pointed at me, so obviously I was in fear of my life. I don't know whether I will return to work as at this time I am thinking I will resign from this garage, as a few cigarettes are not worth my life.'

*

YOU PROBABLY SHOULDN'T judge by appearances, but we'll make an exception in the case of Cody Wilkins, the 25-year-old winner of the award for the most magnificent mobile madness. The police mug shot taken after his arrest shows a white man with unkempt black curly hair, slack jawed and heavy eyelids – not the sort of chap you'd want on your pub quiz team.

It was January 2011, and a storm had caused power cuts in parts of Maryland, including Wilkins' house. So he decided to take his mobile on a burgling spree and *re-charge it in one of his victim's houses*. And then leave it behind when legging it in a hurry – Wilkins, said to be addicted to the painkiller oxycodone, had to jump from a second floor window when the owners returned.

The idiot was later jailed for 26 years and six months, which is a huge stretch by British standards – but before we feel sorry for him, let's hear some more evidence. After being caught Wilkins admitted seven break-ins and eight counts of theft, though detectives suspected that 50 burglaries might be nearer the truth.

One victim, Joanne Lieberman, told *The Washington Post* that Wilkins stole a pair of gold earrings that had been a present from her husband 34 years earlier to mark the birth of their first child. The sentimental jewellery, which was never recovered, was 'the worst thing he could have taken from me'. Clasping her walking stick in both hands, a 79-old-widow testified, 'He took my wedding ring and my engagement ring, he took my mother's wedding ring.'

As the *Post* reported when Wilkins was sentenced after victims spoke of the devastation he caused, 'There was little comedy in court'.

*

IN FEBRUARY 2012, *Police* magazine carried the following snippet, sent in by an officer with the Bedfordshire force. It concerns a man who was nicked for being over the limit after driving home from his local pub. He was in the police station and, having been arrested, one of the officers asked if he'd like to check his text messages before his mobile was taken away. He wasn't too fussed, not even when the officer told him that there was a text from his wife.

'I usually ignore whatever the missus texts me,' he said.

The officer prodded him some more, and eventually the driver was persuaded to have a look at the message.

It read: 'Don't drive home, pigs w8ing 4 u round corner!'

*

LIKE MOST CRIMINAL failures, Paul Nightingale isn't fond of the law. In fact, he even phoned West Midlands Police to lodge a complaint about the force.

The very next day, 29-year-old Nightingale is busy breaking into a house and getting away on a stolen high-value push-bike, when he comes across a brand new Ford Mondeo – with the keys still in the ignition. Not one to look a gift horse in the mouth, Nightingale puts the bike in the boot and drives off in the car.

It gets even better, when he finds the car owner's mobile phone in the glove box. Thinking it must be Christmas, he scrolls through the phone's contacts until he finds the numbers of family members and then uses the phone to text them to demand cash in return for the motor.

He had to use the stolen mobile, because he couldn't find his own.

He couldn't find his own, because he'd dropped it at the scene of the earlier house break-in – which is how the police knew that he was the culprit.

And the phone he dropped was *the same one he'd used when phoning the police the previous day* to complain about their behaviour.

Wolverhampton Crown Court gave him three years.

*

I'VE NEVER COMMITTED a burglary, so I can only speculate, but I'd imagine that the act of breaking into someone else's house would get my adrenalin pumping.

I think I'd be fearful, or excited, or a combination of the two; I'm sure my every sense would be on full alert as I searched the gaff for valuables, a keen ear listening for any sign of occupants or the police.

What I *wouldn't* do is fall asleep.

But then, I'm not John 'Goldilocks' Harrison.

Harrison broke into Jill Norris's empty house one night and started ransacking the place. But he got tired and decided to go for a little lie down. Well, it couldn't hurt, could it? Jill, who'd been out for the night, came back home at 5am to find the 16-year-old tucked up under her duvet. She woke him up and Harrison ran out of the door with £600 worth of jewellery, but not before Jill had got a good look at him.

Itemising his haul, *The Daily Record* reported that it included a gold pocket watch, gold chains, a gold lighter, two silver necklaces, a string of pearls, a wallet, three mobile phones and a tub of hair gel. (*Hair gel?*)

The recidivist thug (his convictions include assault and resisting arrest, and he had been released on bail just a few hours before the break-in) had previously provoked outrage when a court lifted a curfew so that he could go on holiday abroad with his family. There's an unhappy fairytale ending here, too: Perth Sheriff's Court took a lenient view of his bungled burglary and put him on probation.

*

FOR SOME REASON best known to himself, Gary Harrop popped 11 valium tablets before breaking into a house in Taunton, Somerset. The sedatives started kicking in while he was inside, but he pressed on manfully, struggling outside with one haul of loot... Well, *sort of:* he left most of it scattered in the back garden and an alley as he staggered around like a punch-drunk boxer. But he went back for more, and it was then that the valium really ramped up, with the result that he fell stone asleep on the conservatory floor, clutching a load of DVDs.

That's where he was found by homeowner Nicola Phillips, who was alerted when her dog Tyson started barking.

'She crept back upstairs to wake up her boyfriend Dave who went downstairs with a baseball bat and prodded him,' ran the version of the story in *The Daily Express* in August 2011.

I love that word 'prodded': I think most of us would have been tempted to give Harrop a damn good prodding if we found him in our homes, but Dave must be a very forgiving and gentle chap, because *his* prodding was so gentle as to produce no response. So the couple called the police.

Harrop, a 29-year-old 'recovering' heroin addict, was sentenced to 15 months in jail.

*

NOT ALL SUCH STORIES are entirely amusing. William Brown, 61, dozed off in front of his television one night in March 2010, only to awake at 1am to find a burglar standing over him with a machete and a lump hammer.

Ashley Jordan, 24, ordered Mr Brown to hand over whatever money he had to hand, but was not happy with the £50 that the terrified man found by rummaging through his pockets and drawers. Jordan spotted a building society savings book, which seemed more promising. He told Mr Brown that the following morning he'd be marched to the building society so that he could empty the account.

Jordan then settled himself down on the sofa to wait for morning. Unfortunately, for him, he soon drifted off to sleep, giving Mr Brown the chance to creep to a neighbour's house in Solihull, West Midlands, and raise the alarm.

Jordan, whose previous convictions include robbery and burglary, was still asleep when the police arrived to arrest him.

*

RICHARD PARSONS WAS another dozy burglar who was incapable of keeping quiet or staying awake.

He caused £1,500-worth of damage by smashing his way into a home in Kentish Town, north London. He first tried the door, but when that failed he went in through the bay windows, thus ensuring that the neighbours were fully alerted. The 37-year-old stuffed his pockets with valuables before having a kip in an upstairs bedroom, where the police found him.

There is a bizarre postscript recorded by *The Square Mile News*:

> Luckless Parsons' misfortune continued with an embarrassing medical condition forcing him to wear a nappy while on remand at Wandsworth Prison and being at the mercy of teasing inmates during showers.

*

IT'S MUCH THE same story with Robert Erdei. Made lot of noise shifting rubbish bins while breaking into a house in Barnet, north London, then curled up for a nap under a duvet, which is where he was found by a police dog called 'Led Zeppelin'. A police spokesman with a sense of humour said, 'A duvet is no match for Led Zeppelin. He was caught red-handed undercover.'

The 36-year-old, who had already served a 15-month sentence for burglary, got another four years.

*

AT LEAST ROMAN Rebosz managed to make it out of the house he had broken into, in Reading, Berks, in June 2010.

But he didn't get very far.

Having drunk a bottle of vodka and some wine, he made off with a phone. After weaving his way down the road, the 42-year-old collapsed on an old sofa which had been dumped in a nearby street. The phone was still in his pocket when the bobbies woke him up.

*

FINALLY, ONE UNNAMED and amateurish Austrian picked a particularly unusual place to fall asleep – a coffin. In January 2011, *The Austrian Times* reported:

> THE MAN, whose identity was withheld by police in Vienna, broke into an undertaker's in Penzing district on Tuesday night. Undertaker Heinrich Altbart discovered the man fast asleep in one of the coffins the next morning. The 25-year-old intruder reportedly nodded off after having emptied a bottle of red wine he discovered in a wardrobe. Altbart, who took a picture of the napping would-be robber, said today the man caused 'substantial damage' by smashing the front door of his office.

The Vienna case is not unique. *The Huffington Post* reports that police in Bristol, Tennessee, were called to a funeral home where workers found two intruders sleeping inside caskets. One escaped, but police caught and arrested Barrett Lance Hartsock, who was charged with burglary and vandalism over $1,000. Police said there was more than $9,000 in damage done to the caskets the two men were sleeping in.

*

DJ LEE ANTHONY MROSZAK broadcast his crime – literally.

The New Yorker had taken part in Operation Desert Storm in 1990, when he was part of the 82nd Airborne.

In 2004, now a disc jockey, he announced on air that he hadn't filed a tax return in years and would not be doing so until the US government cured his Gulf War Syndrome.

An employee of the Internal Revenue Service happened to be listening, with the result that Mroszak was sentenced to a year in prison and had to pay all his outstanding taxes.

*

ACCORDING TO MY dictionary, 'disguise' is a verb meaning to modify the appearance or manner in order to conceal the identity of oneself, someone, or something.

Its purpose is somewhat defeated if a criminal removes said disguise while still in the shop he's robbing.

Isn't it, Lorenzo Mason?

Mason is a spectacular lamebrain who ended up with a five-year sentence because he removed the scarf covering his face before leaving the bookies that he'd just held up at gunpoint. The resulting CCTV footage, released by Greater Manchester Police, is very instructive. From a camera behind the counter pointing into the shop, first we see Lorenzo, 21, stride up to the counter, dark Adidas hoodie over his head, and poke a handgun through the glass grill.

A terrified shop assistant holds up her hands before disappearing briefly from view, returning again to hand over money to the thug, who had told her: 'Give me all the money. I want all the notes. Don't move and don't touch anything.'

A contradictory order, but we won't quibble with that – not when there's much greater idiocy awaiting.

Mason also grabs a tray of coins, but knocks it over; he then briefly disappears from view as he bends down and scrabbles around on the floor for a few extra quid to add to the £620 in notes that he's been given. Next, the action switches to a camera by the shop door, and a much clearer image of the robber. But there's not much to go on, as there's hardly any face on view: male, black, could be anywhere from 15 to 50.

That's also a reasonable estimate of his IQ, because he seems to change his mind about walking straight out into the street and turns back into the shop, with his back to the camera. It's not obvious for a few seconds what he's doing, but then it all becomes clear. He's removed the scarf from his face, presumably worried that his disguise might arouse suspicion among people passers-by. And, in the process, he gives camera number two an absolutely perfect shot of his face.

Police circulated the photograph and it was recognised by Mason's mother, who urged the idiot to hand himself in.

In October 2010, Manchester Crown Court heard that he had a 'shocking record', including numerous previous convictions for robbery. He's clearly a man who keeps lovely company, because in mitigation it was said that he carried out the raid after receiving a threatening phone call from a drug dealer earlier that day.

In addition, said his lawyer, 'A lack of education and help whilst in prison meant he was unprepared for freedom when he was released.'

Ah, so it wasn't his fault, then. How unusual.

*

THE GANG OF ARMED robbers who raided a village post office in Scotland did keep their disguises on.

Just about.

The trio – John Anderson, 39, Christopher Dailly, 38, and his 35-year-old brother Steven Dailly – were armed with a knife and a hammer when they attacked the post office in Howwood, west of Paisley, in November 2010.

Once inside the building, dozy Dailly major lifted up the hat he was using to cover part of his face, in full view of a CCTV camera, to get a better look around the shop. Meanwhile, Anderson was recognised by 58-year-old postmistress Linda Smith even without removing his disguise.

It all made little difference, because their ugly mugs had already been caught on camera before the raid even began.

When they had arrived at the post office there was a woman waiting at the bus stop outside, so they decided to kick their heels until she left. At that point, they were obviously not yet wearing their disguises because even they had worked out that that would have aroused suspicion.

As *The Paisley Daily Express* reported, 'What they didn't realise was that the Arriva bus the woman had boarded had a CCTV camera installed, and they were caught on its camera.'

And even without the pictures, the woman bus passenger was later able to give police accurate descriptions of the three men who she thought had been acting oddly.

The bus came and went with its incriminating evidence and the gang piled into the post office. But the building had been the subject of a previous robbery and had a security screen and door fitted. The gang's efforts to smash their way through the barricades were in vain and they fled empty-handed.

When police later searched the home where the Dailly brothers lived, they found the distinctive jackets they had been wearing during the raid. Anderson subsequently got eight years, the Dailly brothers seven years apiece. Christopher Dailly, who was out on licence at the time of the cack-handed robbery, was ordered to serve the remaining four years of a previous sentence before beginning his latest jail term.

Lord Turnbull told them, 'You have very, very serious records. I have to deal severely with this in order to protect the public.'

In mitigation – lacking, as ever, in originality – the court heard that all three had addiction problems.

*

ROBBER TAZVIONA BHEBE'S disguise consisted of a pair of baggy grey underpants. With an eye peering out through one of the leg holes and his nose stuck in the crotch, the beknickered nicker (sorry) tried to hold up a convenience store in Sutton, Surrey, with a knife.

Here's a brief (sorry again) list of what went wrong.

1. Enough of his face was visible to be clearly caught on the shop's CCTV.

2. Shop assistant Hari Mahalingham put up stiff resistance, bashing the crook over the head with an advertising board, after first pleading with him not to be such an idiot. 'I tried to talk him out of it, telling him it was a bad idea and he would regret it, but he wouldn't listen,' said Hari.

3. As he fled, Bhebe pulled off the pants, but was immediately recognised by people outside – not surprising, as he lived just around the corner.

In April 2012, he was jailed for three years at Croydon Crown Court after pleading guilty to robbery.

A police spokesman said, 'It's fair to say that this man is not a master of disguise. But this lack of sophistication should not detract from what was a serious offence. He threatened a shop assistant with a knife and it is important that he has been brought to justice.'

*

WHILE IT'S IMPORTANT that a disguise should conceal a robber's appearance, it should also be functional. A Gumby costume is not functional.

(Unknown, I think, in Britain, Gumby is a popular cartoon character in the United States – like a green stick of chewing gum with big smiley face, thin bendy arms and wide floppy legs.)

Yet a man in a Gumby costume attempted to rob a 7-Eleven in California, as explained by San Diego Police spokesman Detective Gary Hassen in September 2011.

'When the clerk thought that the hold-up was a joke,' said Hassen. 'Gumby told him, "You don't think it's a robbery? Let me show you my gun."'

He then experienced a 'costume malfunction' and could not fit his hand into his pocket. As the store assistant waited, he eventually managed to force his way into the pocket, but instead of a gun he pulled out 26 cents in change and spilled it across the floor. Gumby then fled to join an accomplice who was waiting in a mini-van outside the store.

At time of writing, he was still at large.

Although the police are treating the episode as an attempted robbery and not a prank, not everyone is so sure. 'After their getaway, the store clerk was still not certain an attempted robbery had occurred and did not call police,' reported Reuters. 'The store manager, who arrived later that morning, reported the incident.'

That means this robbery – if that's what it was – is probably unique in the chronicles of incompetent crime, in that it was so inept that we can't even be sure that it *was* a crime.

*

WILLIAM STEWART WAS jailed for 45 months, with the judge, Lord McEwan, saying that his robbery was 'doomed to fail' from the beginning.

There wasn't much wrong with the balaclava worn by Stewart. According to every account I've seen, it hid his features well enough. But that didn't stop him being instantly recognised, because he made the basic mistake of robbing a local store – and he had a distinctive stutter, something no mask could disguise.

The High Court in Edinburgh heard in November 2011 how 41-year-old Stewart had used a knife to rob the Farmfoods store in Castlemilk, Glasgow. He often came into the shop, and would speak to workers. When he demanded staff hand over the cash, he started to stutter and was instantly identified.

He escaped with £108, but didn't get very far because his car became stuck in snow. He was arrested the same day.

Even without the stutter, it's doubtful that Stewart would have escaped detection. He'd spent so long hanging around the shop earlier in the day without wearing the balaclava that staff would have known exactly who the man in the mask was, because the rest of his clothes were unchanged.

In mitigation, the court heard that Stewart, who had gone to a nearby pharmacists to get methadone in the morning, was depressed over the death of his father and wasn't feeling well when he carried out the robbery.

'It was a self-destructive impulse,' said his lawyer. 'He said he felt as if he wanted to do something daft.'

In which case, mission accomplished.

*

ROBBER KEVIN BENNETT had a voice that – while not quite as distinctive as William Stewart's stutter – was still easily recognised by the shopkeeper, Majid Rusal, whom he was attempting to rob.

Mind you, even without the voice, Bennett's disguise was so laughably hopeless that he was always likely to be identifiable.

The 19-year-old loser – already on probation and under a community service order – used a knife to hold up a store in the village of Caldercruix, near Airdrie, one December night. He had his hood up, and a scarf wrapped round his face, and made off with £300 in £20 notes.

But he was regular customer, and in May 2011 Prosecutor Pino di Emidio told the High Court in Glasgow, 'Mr Rusal immediately recognised him by his voice. Then the scarf fell, and he could see the face. This was a person that he knew.'

Police arrested Bennett close to his home, his pocket still full of the stolen notes. Despite being caught with the money, and despite knowing that he'd been recognised in the shop, the halfwit tried to maintain his innocence, saying the money had been given to him by his father.

Bennett got three years and nine months in jail. Judge Lord Turnbull said the offence was of 'the most serious nature' and added, 'It is the duty of the courts to protect shopkeepers and others who through nothing other than hard work provide a service to the rest of the community.'

In mitigation, the court heard that Bennett took full responsibility for his actions. Wasn't he supposed to blame heroin addiction?

*

ROBBER ROBERT WHEATLEY held up a branch of the Cambridge Building Society with a crude homemade device – two short pipes taped together that were supposed to look like a gun when held inside a plastic bag. His disguise consisted of sunglasses and a scarf, and he ordered staff to put money into the two Co-op bags that he handed over.

But Wheatley had not been wearing the disguise when he was caught on CCTV a few minutes earlier obtaining the bags from the Co-op a few doors down the same street. Even without that evidence, the disguise was so flimsy that Wheatley was immediately recognised by staff in the building society – *where he had an account*. He was arrested within the hour.

Sara Walker, prosecuting at Cambridge Crown Court in August 2010, said a cashier recognised him straight away.

The 35-year-old, who had 31 convictions for 74 offences, said he tried to rob the building society because he was 'fed up with being skint' and wanted money to buy drugs.

His lawyer told the court, 'It was not the most sophisticated of robberies.'

*

ACCORDING TO *THE Daily Mail*, this was 'Britain's most useless gang', and it may have a point.

In March 2012, along with most other newspapers, the *Mail* reported that five men had left a trail of destruction after smashing their way into seven cash machines *but failing to steal a single penny*.

The gang used equipment ranging from sledgehammers to industrial power tools, and they did get quite *close* to some money on more than one occasion – only to set it on fire with blowtorches.

In one raid, at a Tesco Express at Larkfield in Kent, they missed £140,000 which was there for taking inside an open cash point.

During another, they were so noisy that they woke people living nearby and were forced to run off.

After yet another, they tried to hide behind bins at a Co-op in Burgess Hill, West Sussex, but were spotted.

The talentless thieves were all jailed after a trial at Canterbury Crown Court. Dominic Connolly, prosecuting, said, 'These defendants were part of a team that, over a period of three weeks, travelled to various locations in the south east of England in order to attack commercial premises that housed ATMs in order to steal the contents. However, despite their extensive efforts, no money was actually obtained.'

The Mirror ran this with the headline 'Hole in the wally gang.'

Not that the gang members are the only idiots in this saga. The ringleader, 27-year-old James Whitlock of no fixed abode, committed the crimes when he was supposed to be in jail, serving a 33-month sentence for theft. He had been wrongly transferred to a low-security prison, escaped and went on to carry out the ATM fiasco.

*

A LOVELY PRESS release from West Midlands Police in October 2010 described how a convicted burglar failed to appear in court for his sentencing 'because he didn't want to spend the weekend locked up'.

Isiah Beard had been due before Warwick Crown Court on September 30, but didn't turn up. He was arrested four days later and jailed for 18 months.

Detective Constable Steve Tarver, said, 'Officers executed a warrant at an address frequented by Beard and found him relaxing in the living room. He was perfectly calm and simply said he didn't turn-up for sentence as he didn't want to spend the weekend in the cells.'

The 21-year-old had been involved in two very unsubtle burglaries. In one, he'd kicked down the front door of a property in

Chelmsley Wood, to the east of Birmingham, and stolen £200. In the other, he was among a gang that broke into another Chelmsley Wood property and stole a laptop, digital camera and a games console.

But how had he been caught? After all, the CCTV footage shows him wearing a balaclava as he fled the scene. Thing is, the idiot wasn't wearing the balaclava when he *entered* the flats, and the cameras got a nice, clear shot of his face.

*

IN CRIME, AS in comedy, timing is everything. A simple rule, but one that was lost on the robber who struck at a Bradford shop, early one February morning in 2012.

Very early.

Too early.

So early, in fact, that not a single customer had been served, and owner Didar Bansal had not even put the float in the till.

A bleary-eyed Mr Bansal was still sorting out the morning papers when he heard a voice demand, 'Give me your bloody money.'

At first, he assumed it was one of his regular customers having a joke, but then he saw that the intruder was wearing a balaclava. 'I haven't got any money,' said Mr Bansal, at which the raider demanded to look in the till. Disappointed to see that it really *was* empty, he then demanded to know where the safe was.

'I don't have a safe,' said Mr Bansal.

The raider took the bag he'd brought with him, presumably expecting to leave with it bulging with cash, and stormed off.

'I don't think he was a professional,' remarked the beautifully understated shopkeeper.

*

ARMED ROBBER JOHN Fulton must have been truly desperate to help the over-worked cops; he left them not one but two lovely pieces of evidence to assist them in their investigations. In fact, his attempt to rob a Glasgow post office was so inept that you wonder whether he genuinely does like prison food.

First, Fulton, 53, decided to fill in a lottery ticket, thereby leaving his fingerprints all over the lotto stand. Then he presented the ticket to the shop assistant, pointed a handgun and demanded money, prompting the embarrassing reply, 'Are you stupid? You're on camera.'

Ah, yes, the ski mask! Only then did Fulton realise that it would be a good idea to pull it down over his face, by which point his ugly mug had already been caught on two CCTV monitors.

The dim crim fled empty-handed when another customer came into the shop. He was jailed for four years in January 2011, his mitigation being that he needed money to pay for his father's funeral – as though (even if true) that would excuse putting an innocent shop worker through such an ordeal.

*

TRISTAN WOOD ALSO left his bag at the scene of a break-in – and it, too, had his name and other personal details inside.

The 37-year-old was piling jewellery, watches and a camera into the bag when owner John Hall returned to his house in Ramsgate, Kent, and saw the front door smashed in. After a tussle, Wood did a runner, abandoning the bag which had his name stitched into the lining. He was found by police hiding behind a nearby tree.

The heroin addict who had been released from a jail sentence shortly before the burglary later claimed that he had nowhere to live and had been looking for a place to sleep. *Right.*

He got 18 months, his defence lawyer telling Canterbury Crown Court: 'He is not a professional burglar.'

You don't say.

*

SIMON CALLAWAY was stopped by the police late one night, as he strolled down the street.

Why did they stop him?

Because he was carrying a pink handbag – something of a giveaway.

The 38-year-old was arrested, convicted of burglary, nine other offences were taken into account, and in November 2011 he was sentenced to 15 months inside, after being described at Swindon Crown Court as a criminal with 'a long list of previous convictions'.

That story puts me in mind of the looter involved in the August 2011 riots who was caught because he was wearing the lady's watch that he'd just stolen from a Manchester jewellery shop. Dale Siddall, 19, also had a stolen ring on his wedding finger and a woman's bracelet in his pocket, plus a jewellery box from a neighbouring store. Both were stripped clean by looters, although Siddall's share of the loot came to only £100.

In sending the 'trainee plasterer' to a Young Offenders' Institution for 16 months, Judge Martin Rudland said, 'It's no good saying you were led on by the rabble – you *were* the rabble.'

*

HERE'S SOME MORE inappropriate riot-wear. This time, the scene is Seattle and the May Day protests of 2012, and one picture in particular made the news. It showed a painfully trendy rioter in black trousers, black top, lavender shirt, purple scarf over his face and pink hairband to keep his hoodie in place. Behind him the words 'Death to Capitalism' have been sprayed on a shop window. So far, so anarchic. But our man is attacking a Nike store, and on his feet are a pair of, yes, Nike trainers. Is that anarchy, or product-placement?

*

BROTHERS KEIRAN and Ryan Keoghan were quick to take advantage of the riots of 2011.

They'd probably have got away scot-free, too – if only they hadn't been so incredibly lazy.

The south London streets around them were ablaze, and – with police keeping a low profile – they had their pick of stores to loot, but decided to rob the '3' mobile phone store *immediately below their own flat*.

Goods worth more than £100,000 were taken, and when police visited their flat, along with others nearby, they found an empty Apple iPad box linked to the store's stock.

Kieran, 27, was already a convicted burglar, and both he and 26-year-old Ryan went down for 18 months.

*

THE EVIDENCE THAT helped catch burglar Joshua Curley was remarkable.

Curley had taken Pam Parker's camera, a laptop, and some irreplaceable family jewellery during a raid on her house in Newport, south Wales. The haul was worth at least a thousand pounds, but the 19-year-old had a cunning plan – why not send Pam a ransom note asking for a relatively small sum in return for the stolen property? Surely she'd pay up rather than involve the cops?

So he sent a note reading, 'Give me £80 to get it back.'

You or I might have typed it, or cut letters out from a newspaper the old-fashioned way.

But then, we wouldn't be in this book.

Curley wrote the note in his own incriminating, distinctive and particularly bad hand-writing, and when Mrs Parker passed it to the police. Detectives – who already suspected Curley – used a handwriting expert to prove that the 'child-like' scribble was his.

In November 2011, he was sentenced to four years after admitting three burglaries and two robberies.

*

HISTORY DOES NOT record what Philip Trapp's hand-writing is like, but he'd be advised to be a bit more careful with his spelling.

The Daily Telegraph thought the following was so funny that it put the story on its front page on March 5, 2012:

> WHEN THE police received a letter from the victim of a dog attack insisting that he did not wish to press charges, something did not ring true.
>
> In fact, the letter had come from the dog's owner, Philip Trapp, who had made a simple, but perhaps understandable, mistake – he misspelt the name of victim Thomas Matangambiri, arousing officers' suspicions.

Guildford Crown Court heard that Trapp, 41, of Tadworth, Surrey, had set his bull terrier on Mr Matangambiri after calling him a 'n*****' on May 6 last year. He claimed that he was shouting the dog's name, 'Trigger', but the judge jailed him for eight months.

*

SOME STERLING AMATEUR detective work, combined with a crucial piece of evidence left at the scene of the crime, led to the conviction of a teenage bicycle thief.

All right, stealing a bike isn't the most serious crime, but it's not nice when it happens to you – and it was particularly unpleasant for David Bradley, who suffered from cancer and needed the bike to get to his doctor's appointments.

The police not being too interested in matters such as this, Mr Bradley's wife Lisa began the search for the culprit by finding an empty can of an energy drink foolishly left behind in their garden shed in Crowthorne, Berkshire.

She then searched for the shop that had sold the can; sure enough, there was one which had CCTV showing a teenager buying it and, a little later, pushing the stolen bike past the shop.

Lisa managed to persuade the shop to hand the images over to her, and then posted them online to get the toerag identified.

He subsequently got a 12-month community order and was ordered to carry out 60 hours of unpaid work.

There was a strange pay-off to this saga, when one commenter on the *Daily Mail* website suggested that posting the pictures of the thief online by Lisa might have meant that she was breaking the Data Protection Act. David Bradley, surely speaking for every sane person in the county, responded: 'Stop worrying about his rights and start thinking about the law abiding citizens.'

*

A THUG WHO TRIED to rob cinema staff at knifepoint was caught after he dropped a bottle of medication with his name on it. Ray Currie, 35, attempted to force open a till after jumping over the counter at a cinema in Glasgow in 2011.

He fled empty-handed and was traced after dropping the medicine. His clumsiness cost him a seven-year sentence, the judge remarking, 'These are, sadly, only the latest in a long line of similar offences for which you have frequently served sentences of imprisonment.'

*

STEPHANIE MORELAND, a shoplifter from Bloomington, Minnesota, stuffed a fur coat worth £5,000 inside her clothing. She was challenged by a suspicious shop assistant, but denied everything and drove off. Her licence plate was passed on to the police, who paid her a visit. They, too, came up blank, and the thief would have got away had cops not found one vital piece on incriminating evidence in her car – the coat hanger, bearing the shop's logo.

In case you're wondering how someone managed to shoplift an item as bulky as a fur coat, ~~Morelard~~ Moreland was so obese that she was able conceal it in her pants. I refer you to Bloomington Police Commander Mark Stehlik, though I'm afraid I struggle to visualise his fur-coat-and-half-knickers explanation: 'She had modified her underwear. She actually cut the rear of the underwear out so that from the back it appeared she was not wearing underwear and then stuffed it down the front.'

I've tried it at home, and I still don't get it.

✳

STILL IN THE STATES, we have a lovely bungled example of what in the UK we'd call 'doing a runner', and Americans refer to as 'dine-and-dash'. According to the *Springfield News-Leader* in Missouri, three women legged it from a branch of Waffle House without paying the $39 bill. The manager said the trio seemed intoxicated or under the influence of drugs, which might be why two of them left their purses behind.

One of the women later returned to the store and demanded the return of the purses, but left again when told to wait for police to arrive. A police report said the purses contained identifying documents, along with what appeared to be a cheque stub from another Waffle House in Arkansas.

Some online comments doubt the veracity of the tale, even though the source is the highly-reputable Associated Press, partly because of the lack of detail, such as the name of the restaurant manager, but mainly because of the apparent impossibility of three people eating $39 worth of waffles. Although, as one commenter observed, 'Have you seen the SIZE of girls nowadays?'

✳

POLICE OFFICER Chad Herndon was in uniform and sitting at a desk in the foyer of the Metropolitan Bank in Little Rock, Arkansas, when a customer walked past him to the counter, and asked a member of staff for directions to the toilets. (I've never been in a bank which has toilets, but that's by the by.)

The customer – one Langston Robins – then walked back past Officer Chad to go what they call in the States 'the restroom'.

Then he passed Chad for the third time and approached the counter again, where he informed the cashier that he was robbing the joint and handed over his gym bag, demanding it be filled with cash.

Chad was surprised, to say the least, by this turn of events.

After all, there was a policeman – Chad – sitting about six feet away, in a policeman's uniform.

At first, Chad assumed he must have misheard, and leaned forward on his chair, hands clasped in his lap, to get a better earful.

At which point, he realised this really *was* a robbery, and quietly moved in behind Robins to arrest him.

There was a scuffle, the pair clattered into some chairs and a desk and Robins managed to escape into the street outside, where he was arrested five minutes later and charged with aggravated robbery, second-degree battery, resisting arrest and fleeing.

*

WILLIAM KELTNER WANTED a new telly – he just didn't want to pay full price.

So the 52-year-old came up with a clever scheme – why not swap the barcode sticker for another, cheaper one?

Not a bad idea, if you ignore the obvious criminality.

But he pushed it a bit too far when he replaced the $228 tag for one which read '$1.17'.

Staff at the Walmart in Abilene, Texas, spotted this without too much bother, and called the police.

*

HOLLY SOLOMON ISN'T a big fan of President Obama, so she wasn't best pleased when he was re-elected at the last US poll.

Perhaps unreasonably, she held her husband Daniel responsible.

Definitely unreasonably, she got into a furious argument with him about it, and then ran him over with her car.

It all started when Mr Solomon, 35, admitted that he hadn't bothered to vote.

Police in Gilbert, Arizona, said witnesses heard a row erupt in a car park. There was a lot of yelling, and then Holly, 28, climbed into her Jeep and started chasing a terrified Daniel.

He tried hiding behind a lamp post, while his angry wife circled him, shouting threats from her window. When he tried to make a run for it, she ran him over, trapping him under the car.

He suffered serious injuries, and Holly was charged with domestic violence and aggravated assault.

As the *Phoenix New Times* pointed out, Daniel's failure to vote was irrelevant, in any case – Arizonans had voted overwhelmingly for Mitt Romney anyway.

*

TEENAGERS KODY THRONSON and Casey Gillette thought all their Christmases had arrived when – while out breaking into vehicles in Fargo, North Dakota – they stumbled across an unlocked car stuffed with goodies.

To make it even better, it was an unmarked *police* car – so the goodies included a bulletproof vest, some handcuffs, a Taser, a police knife, a handheld police radio, and pistol ammunition clips.

Within moments, the pair were horsing around with their booty. There was the predictable posing for photos in the vest, shouting rude things such as 'F*** the police!' down the radio and throwing the knife around. They'd have got away with it all, too, if only Gillette, 18, hadn't thought it a good idea to slap the cuffs on another chum, Joe Tolzmann.

The problem with handcuffs is they're easy to put on – but, by design, hard to get off.

After giggling for a while, the youths realised they hadn't got the keys. They then spent several hours trying to remove them from the unfortunate Tolzmann before he gave up and called the cops, telling them he needed releasing.

The officers who attended quickly realised that the cuffs belonged to one of their colleagues, and the three were arrested.

*

I HAVE NEVER been to Poulsbo in America's Washington State, but I'm told it's very nice.

It's part of a promontory which juts out into the Pacific ocean – and, as such, it ought to be hard to get lost there.

You drive in on Highway 3, you drive out on Highway 3.

How hard can it be?

Ask Jared Persitz.

The 22-year-old from Vancouver, just over the Canadian border, staged a particularly unpleasant raid on a petrol station there early one Christmas Day morning. He threatened staff with a butterfly knife and repeatedly threatened to kill them if they didn't give him some money. One of the employees picked up the phone to call the police, at which Persitz tried – and failed – to cut the phone cable. Then, furious at not being taken seriously, he hurled everything off the counter onto the floor and stormed out into the darkness, empty-handed.

An hour and a half later, the staff noticed a familiar red Honda Accord pull up onto the forecourt. It was Persitz again – only, this time, he hadn't come to rob the joint.

'Excuse me,' he said, 'but can you tell me the way out of this place?'

He had spent the intervening 90 minutes driving aimlessly round Poulsbo, trying and failing to find his way back to Canada.

He was arrested shortly afterwards, and admitted robbery. Sgt Bill Playter, of the town's police department, said, 'I guess he got lost. He's not the brightest bulb in the closet.'

*

EVEN THE MOST law-abiding smokers may sympathise with the story of Dan Griggs.

It was 1am, and he was desperate for a fag. But he didn't have any cash, so he decided to help himself to a few packets at a convenience store.

Sadly, his plan was flawed, in multiple ways.

Firstly, the shop was directly opposite the police station in Lake Station, a suburb of Gary, Indiana.

Secondly, after successfully grabbing the ciggies and skedaddling, he found that his car was locked… with the keys inside.

Thirdly, a shop assistant had followed him, and now he confronted Griggs. Dan said the whole thing was a joke, or a mistake, and that he hadn't actually meant to steal the cigarettes. Unsurprisingly, the man didn't buy this and started yelling for the cops.

Police Lieutenant Mike Stills explained how Griggs then went back into the store, pulled out the telephone wire, and ordered staff to hand over the cash in the till. When they refused, he broke open a lottery machine, stole fifty dollars and legged it again.

Back to the car – which was still locked. Aaaarrrggghhh!

Back to the store, steal a broom, use it to smash the driver's window – as a growing crowd of police officers watch from the station across the road.

Despite all of these setbacks, the valiant thief eventually got into his vehicle, started it and drove off.

Straight into a police car.

He staggered from the vehicle, took to his toes, promptly fell into a ditch, and was arrested.

*

IT SOUNDED LIKE a soft target – surely you're not going to get much resistance if you rob a beauty college, especially if you're armed with a .38 revolver?

That was the basis of Jared Gipson's plan, and at first it worked a treat.

Wearing a handkerchief over his face, the 24-year-old got inside the Blalock Beauty College in Shreveport, Louisiana, and forced principal Dianne Mitchell and 20 of her students and employees to give him their cash and valuables.

'He walked up behind me and said, "This is a hold-up!' said Mrs Mitchell, 53. 'At first, I thought it was someone just playing, but then I saw that big old gun. He said, "Get down big momma!"'

People started handing stuff over, and some of the students began crying. This irritated Gipson, who told one of the sobbing women she would be 'the first to go'.

When he was satisfied that he had everything he could take, Gipson made a run for the door.

That's when it all went wrong.

Mrs Mitchell stuck out a leg and tripped him, and he crashed to the floor, dropping his gun. Before he had time to think, he found himself submerged under a spitting, scratching, punching, human tidal wave. He was so badly beaten – with curling tongues, hairdryers and a table leg – that he was left crying, bleeding and begging for help from the police.

They duly arrived, took him to Shreveport's LSU Hospital where he was given 21 stitches, and then booked him into jail.

He was looking at up to 203 years in chokey, but his victims asked the judge to go easy on him. Caddo District Judge Scott Crichton bowed to their wishes, and gave Gipson a mere 25 years, reported the Associated Press.

The robber said that a friend had told him that the women at Blalock's would be easy prey. 'That was obviously some really, really bad advice,' said the judge.

Sharon Blalock, owner of the school, put it succinctly: 'They just whooped the hell out of him.'

*

AS HE WAS being charged with armed robbery and aggravated unlawful restraint, Andre Mitchell must have wondered where it had all gone wrong.

On paper, that morning's job had looked like a piece of cake.

The victim was 60 years old, and Mitchell was a fit 20-year-old.

Plus, he had a pair of pistols.

All he had to do was lie in wait for the old guy, jump into his car and force him to drive around the place, cashing cheques at bank drive-throughs (they have these in the States).

As so often, things started well. Wearing a black mask, he ambushed Roger Molski – who happened to be the mayor of Flossmoor, Illinois – at 6.15am, as he was climbing out of his Lincoln Continental to open his insurance office for the day. Brandishing his guns – which were very convincing fakes – Mitchell forced the older man back into the car, and demanded money.

'He said no-one would get hurt if I cooperated,' said Mr Molski. 'I offered him the car but he rejected it. He said he needed $10,000.'

It was now 6.20am, and about three hours before the banks actually opened. There was nothing for it but to drive around, waiting. At one point, he talked his captor into going to McDonald's for breakfast. He hoped that the drive-through staff there might find it odd that he had a masked man in his back seat, and call the cops, but all that happened was the mayor had a coffee and bought Mitchell a bacon-and-egg McMuffin.

The banks opened, and Mr Molski withdrew $2,000 from two of them. 'But he wanted more,' he said.

When the mayor tried to cash a third check at the Bank of Homewood, the teller refused it and asked Molski to come inside.

This was the turning point of the day, and Andre Mitchell's life.

Luckily, the mayor was intelligent and his tormentor was thick, and now he used this to his advantage.

'Er, I need to go inside,' he said. 'It would be better if I went on my own.'

Mitchell, seeing no problem with this, leaned forward and warned the mayor to make sure he was back within 15 minutes, tops.

What happened next is entirely predictable to all but the very stupid. 'I went in and yelled, "Quick! Lock the doors and call 911. I'm being robbed!"' said Mr Molski.

Before long, the distant wail of sirens alerted even the terminally dumb Mitchell to the reality of his situation, and he fled. He was arrested later that day.

*

THE FLORIDA ROBBER had it all worked out.

He'd stroll into the Jacksonville branch of the First Union Bank and hand over a note saying that he had a bag full of dynamite which he'd set off if they didn't hand him a bag full of cash.

It worked, too

Until the clerk turned over the note, and found that it was written *on the back of an arrest report*, for an assault on a police officer four days earlier.

Of all the bits of paper he could have chosen, Osman Brown, 19, had used perhaps the worst possible one.

The cops picked him up not far from the bank.

*

TO CALL THE police asking if you can buy crack from them once is careless; to do it three times is just plain stupid.

Meet Amy Logue of Ashland, Ohio. The 27-year-old dialled what she thought was her dealer's number and got through to the cops.

Even when the dispatcher answered her call, 'Ontario Police… how may I help you?', Logue tried to arrange an $80 buy at a disused petrol station.

NBC TV carried a transcript of one of the farcical calls:

> Logue: 'Do you have any drugs?'
> Police: 'Any *what*?'
> Logue: 'Drugs, crack?'
> Police: 'Er… probably.'
> Logue: 'Got anything good?'

Once they had realised it wasn't a prank call, the police agreed to meet her – though she switched the location to a nearby McDonald's 'because she didn't want to seem too obvious or suspicious,' Lieutenant Rob Griefenstine of the Ontario police told the United Press.

When detectives arrived, they gave Logue plenty of chance to back out. A tape picked up the following exchange:

> Officer: 'How do I know you ain't a cop, huh?'
> Logue: 'How do *you* know *I* ain't a cop?'

She was arrested and initially charged with a felony, but the charges were dropped. 'It's the worst case of a misdialled phone number I've ever seen,' said Lt Griefenstine. 'It did not go to court. Although a clear violation of the law, our law director elected not to pursue the case and it was therefore never prosecuted.'

*

ARLINA ALVES WENT one better, and actually flagged down a passing uniformed cop to ask for his help in getting her a 'fix' of heroin.

Patrolman Raymond Siko was taken aback, to say the least.

Shamokin, Pennsylvania's *News Item* newspaper reported in March 2013 how Mr Siko explained that he was a police officer, to which she replied, 'That's even better, because you probably have some heroin at the station that you have taken off people. I only need one bag.'

The 49-year-old was booked on charges of being drunk and disorderly.

*

MANNERS MAKETH THE man, but not the bank robber.

Rob Howell went into the branch of Barclays in Pontypridd, south Wales, said, 'Can I see the manager, please?' and slipped a note under the glass screen.

It read, 'Give me the money, please. I've got a knife.'

Then he stood to one side and waited patiently for the manager to come over, as the teller served other customers.

He was still waiting 10 minutes later when police arrived to arrest him, Merthyr Crown Court heard.

Howell, 61, from Pontypridd, admitted attempted robbery.

*

EMERSON MOORE JR was arrested for drunken driving and bailed to appear in court the next day.

When he showed up at the court in Muhlenberg, Pennsylvania, he saw the officer who had arrested him and a row blew up between them. During the argument, the officer – Trooper Roberto Soto – smelled alcohol on 46-year-old Moore's breath.

Given that he had driven himself to court, this was not a good thing. He was breath-tested, found to be over the limit again, had his bail revoked and was sent to jail.

'You don't show up drunk for a preliminary hearing, especially when it's a drunk-driving case,' said the judge, District Justice Dean Patton. 'I asked him what he was thinking and he said, "You told me I could drink at home."'

*

RICHARD BROWN WAS in enough trouble when he appeared before Judge Patrick Carroll on charges of robbing a shop in West Haven, Connecticut.

He was already looking at 10½ years for that offence when the judge reprimanded him for his surly attitude, and ordered him to say 'Yes, sir' when addressing the court.

At that, the simpleton blew his top.

Standing up, he dropped his prison-issue trousers, turned around and mooned the bench, yelling, 'Sir? Kiss my ass, sir!'

Ooops.

Better make that *11½* years.

*

WHEN ANCIENT CHINESE artefacts worth £2 million were pinched from a museum in a daring midnight raid, it looked to be the work of a highly-experienced gang of thieves – probably with shadowy connections to the underground international market in stolen antiquities.

It wasn't.

It was the work of a pair of dummies from Walsall, Lee Wildman and Adrian Stanton, and it was later described by a judge as 'a complete farce'.

The two managed to get into Durham University's Oriental Museum in April 2012 by chiselling a hole in the wall, and made off with the first things they found, which just happened to be an 18th century jade bowl and a Dehua porcelain figurine.

But then they panicked, worried that they might have been heard, and hid their treasure on some waste ground.

The idea was that they'd come back in a day or two to retrieve it, but when they came back they couldn't remember where they had left the booty.

Witnesses saw Wildman pacing up and down on the waste land, shouting into his phone and looking 'agitated', Newcastle Crown Court heard.

Police picked them up shortly afterwards.

Judge Christopher Prince, jailing Wildman, 35, and Stanton, 32, for nine and eight years respectively, said, 'This is not an offence that can be described as sophisticated. There were elements that reduced it to complete farce. Lawyers with many years' experience have not seen a case where thieves have hidden property where they just could not find it afterwards – let alone property of this cultural importance and enormous value.'

*

SADLY, THEY AREN'T the only idiots in this line of work.

When a collection of art worth millions of pounds was stolen from a transport lorry parked in a warehouse in Madrid in November 2010, the police naturally assumed they were looking for a gang of professionals. After all, the haul included a Picasso and a number of pieces by the renowned Basque sculptor, Eduardo Chillida. Probably an inside job, reckoned detectives, and the owners would be lucky to see their treasures again. They'd soon be adorning the flats of unscrupulous super-rich collectors on the other side of the world.

Until a few days later, when one of the gang turned up at a nearby scrapyard and tried to flog a £675,000 sculpture for £25.

The cops were called, and the whole lot was found, intact, in a lock-up near the industrial estate from where they were stolen.

The police – who are still looking for the thieves – reconsidered their initial theory. 'It now appears more likely that we are dealing with amateurs,' said a spokesman.

*

AND THEN THERE is John Maughan, who snatched a Stradivarius violin worth £1.2 million and tried to sell it for £100.

Maughan pinched the violin from the South Korean violinist Min-Jin Kym as she put it down at London's Euston station while buying a sarnie at Pret A Manger.

Not being the musical type, Maughan had no idea what he'd got his hands on – the bow *alone* was worth £62,500.

He did a bit of online research, but was just as clueless afterwards as before, and he ended up offering it to a stranger in an internet café.

The guy turned down their offer, saying, 'No thanks. My daughter's already got a recorder.'

Maughan was identified stealing the violin on CCTV images as two teenage accomplices distracted her and the staff, and walking out with it. Prosecutor Mark James-Dawson told Southward Crown Court, 'The next day the three defendants were in an internet café in Tottenham Court Road. They were researching the word "Stradivarius" and 1698, the year the violin was made. We know this because a witness was on a computer next to them. They entered into a discussion with him and tried to sell it to him at a price of £100. He doesn't buy it because his daughter has a recorder already.'

Dublin-born Maughan, 30, a serial thief with over 40 different aliases, 26 different dates of birth and 123 previous convictions, got four-and-a-half years in jail.

*

FROM NO DISGUISE, to *too much* disguise.

Thomas Clark hatched what he thought was a brilliant plan to rob a building society – he would pose as a wheelchair-bound woman.

It didn't go well.

For starters, Clark was sporting several days' stubble underneath the ill-fitting black wig he was wearing when his mate and fellow genius Martin Collins pushed him in through the main door of the Permanent TSB in Stillorgan, south Dublin.

So manager Michael Doyle was immediately suspicious.

He was waiting to meet the pair because Collins had made an appointment, saying that he was caring for a woman who had been awarded €2.9 million in damages and wanted to invest it.

Mr Doyle's suspicions only grew when Collins carefully positioned the wheelchair facing the door.

Clark, 42, got out of the wheelchair and produced what Mr Doyle thought, at first, was a shotgun and shouted, 'Get down on the floor!'

But the manager quickly realised the weapon was an imitation, and when Collins, 21, produced a similar weapon he shouted at them, 'Would you ever f*** off?', before telling them to, 'Stop being stupid!'

Alas, this was an instruction which the pair were ill-equipped to carry out.

Collins hit Mr Doyle on the back of the leg, and then the pair of them fled society empty-handed. The Gardaí arrested them a short time later.

Both men pleaded guilty at Dublin Circuit Criminal Court to attempted robbery. Clark got six years and Collins three.

*

I DON'T THINK the following is really trying.

In fact, I'm not sure it even counts as a disguise.

Police stopped two men they believed were planning a burglary in Iowa around Halloween 2009.

They instantly recognised the pair from the description they'd been given. That's because Matthew McNelly, 23, and Joey Miller, 20, didn't wear balaclavas, or stockings, or ski masks, or anything else: they simply scrawled black marker pen all over their faces. This did nothing to hide their identities, it just made them look like two very dim blokes who'd gone a bit mad with a felt tip.

Asked how officers knew that the pair were their culprits when that their car was pulled over, Police Chief Jeff Cayler told CNN, 'We're very skilled investigators.'

If you think that's sarcastic, it's nothing compared to Willie Geist, a presenter on US channel MSNBC: 'Some people say America's youth is fatter, dumber and more apathetic than ever. They say kids today are a bunch of lazy, drooling video game addicts destined to die of overdoses from Taco Bell and Red Bull. I disagree generally, but every so often there's a case that makes you wonder.'

After running through the details of the case, Geist goes on: 'How about a Halloween mask? They're everywhere right now. It's not that hard. Permanent marker is literally the very last thing you would want to use to hide your identity while committing a crime. Or is it duct tape? Remember this guy from the Ashland, Kentucky, chapter of Mensa [he shows an extraordinary picture of a man's head and face wrapped in silver tape with some bloody lips and one swollen eye showing through] who tried to hold up a liquor store with his head wrapped in duct tape so he wouldn't be recognised?

'Well, this method also proved ineffective, as the would-be criminal couldn't see out of his own disguise. After the store clerk

got done laughing at the guy he beat the crap out of him. America, we can do better. Let's work together to teach the next generation of burglars and thieves that permanent marker and duct tape are no way to disguise oneself for a home invasion and no way to lead this great country into the new century.'

As it happened, a court in Carroll, Iowa, later decided that the burglary charges against McNelly and Miller wouldn't stick because when they kicked at the apartment door they could have been intending to scare the occupant rather than break in. But they remain guilty of stupidity, Magistrate Chris Polking calling their escapade, 'Ill-conceived and ill-advised, to an extent that is difficult to express adequately.'

*

MOST CRIME IS committed by men, but that doesn't mean there aren't plenty of stupid female criminals out there.

Like Hannah Sabata, who carried out a series of thefts and robberies – and then *posted a YouTube video of herself bragging about it*.

Perhaps someone had warned the 19-year-old not to actually *say* anything, because, you know, that might be used against her in evidence.

But although she doesn't speak a word during the eight-minute film, that's a bit of a moot point because in the YouTube description she calls herself 'Bank Robber Chick' and adds the following:

> I just stole a car and robbed a bank. Now I'm rich, I can
> pay off my college financial aid and tomorrow I'm going
> for a shopping spree. Bite me. I love GREENDAY!

For non-hep cats, Greenday are an American popular music recording combo, and the video is set to one of their songs, *Warning*.

Viewers can see her grinning as she holds up handwritten signs saying thing like, 'I stole a car!' and 'Then I robbed a bank!!', while brandishing a gun and a bag of marijuana, and fanning out wads of cash.

To help the cops just a little more, she's still wearing the clothes in which she carried out her alleged crimes.

She's grinning throughout, and it's all very amusing – though perhaps not for the staff at the Waco, Nebraska branch of the Cornerstone Bank, into which she went in November 2012.

Having arrived there in a stolen Pontiac Grand Am sports car, which she described as 'shiny', she handed them a note saying, 'You are being robbed! NO ALARMS OR LOCKS OR PHONES or INK BAGS! I have a loaded gun. You have 2 minutes.'

Sabata quickly generated a million YouTube hits, and found legions of adoring Generation Y fans, delighted that she was sticking it to The Man.

Unfortunately, the impressive evidence trail she had left rapidly led to her apprehension, and her smile faded somewhat in June 2013 when she was jailed for between 10 and 20 years by a York County judge.

*

BY DEFINITION, CRIMINALS love free stuff.

Canny cops in Derbyshire turned this against them by sending letters to dozens of wanted crims in their county, telling them the good news – they had each won a free crate of beer!

All they had to do to collect their booze was to ring a marketing company.

Which 19 of the thickest – on the run from justice after carrying out crimes including burglary, robbery and serious sex offences – duly did.

Unfortunately, the number actually went through to an office at Chesterfield police station, where they were given instructions as to when and where to collect.

And when they turned up, they got a nasty surprise.

Chief Inspector Graham McLaughlin, who led the November 2011 operation, told *The Sunday Mercury* (which ran the story under the amusing headline 'A Bitter Blow'), 'These people have managed to evade arrest for some time, so we have used different tactics to find them.'

*

EVEN I DON'T advocate death sentences for thieves – but that's just what one particularly stupid gang may have inflicted on themselves.

Steven Cameron and his mates decided to pinch the steel beams supporting a farmer's barn in Blairgowrie, Perthshire, in March 2011.

The idea was to get a few quid for them from a scrap metal merchant.

But they may have got rather more than they bargained for.

Firstly, they made so much noise, and created such a dust cloud, that they were caught red-handed.

That was only a small part of their problem. Much worse was the fact that the beams were clad in asbestos – which is deadly when breathed in.

And the four fools had spent an hour or so choking in that dust cloud.

At Perth Sheriff's Court, Sheriff Kenneth McGowan told ringleader Cameron, 'This was not exactly the crime of the century. It seems inevitable you were going to be caught, if not red-handed, then immediately afterwards. Even more significant than that is that you have undoubtedly exposed yourself to asbestos. I understand that the contamination effect is a one-shot deal. All you require is one exposure in your lifetime and it can have very grave consequences for your health. That is a very great concern for you.'

Perhaps that is why McGowan treated the men so lightly. Cameron was fined only £225 – for causing damage that would cost £80,000 to repair – and the other three were allowed to walk from the court after the prosecution dropped charges against them because Cameron had admitted he was the 'brains' of the scheme.

*

JUDGES SEE AN awful lot of stupid criminals, so when one of them describes a man as 'ranking amongst the all-time stupidest criminals to come before the courts' we should sit up and take notice.

That was how Judge Donagh McDonagh described Gary Byrne, after a botched armed robbery where he and his gang had to be rescued by the fire brigade.

Byrne, 30, led a heist on a gold storage business in Dublin, assisted by Ian Jordan, 33, and Aidan Murphy, 32.

It was no laughing matter for the staff, who were threatened with a gun and bound and gagged.

In fact, it was not funny at all – until they were nearly finished.

That was the moment when Byrne took it into his head to leave with the loot, and *lock the shutters behind him*, leaving Jordan and Murphy trapped inside with the two terrified workers.

Byrne had taken the keys, too, and just scarpered. His accomplices spent an hour or so discovering that it's just as hard to get *out* of a locked gold vault as in, and then – picture their faces – called the fire brigade.

They duly arrived and cut the shutters open – and the disconsolate pair walked out into the arms of the waiting police. They soon rounded Byrne up, too. He got seven years, and the others five apiece.

Judge McDonagh said it was 'one of the most farcical cases in recent criminal history in Dublin.'

'One thing is for sure,' he added. 'Byrne's ineptitude and stupidity does not, in any way, reduce his culpability.'

*

IF I WERE A MAJOR league drug dealer, I'd do as little as possible to attract the attention of the cops.

Adopt a low profile, keep my nose clean, that sort of thing.

What I *wouldn't* do is allow a stolen iPad – with all that fancy Apple tracking software in it – to come into the apartment where I was warehousing $34 million-worth of methamphetamine for a Mexican cartel.

But then, I'm not *that* stupid.

The police were only looking for the stolen tablet when they tracked it to the well-kept home in San Jose, California, using its built-in GPS.

Even when they knocked on the door, they could *still* have been sent packing – they didn't have a search warrant.

Instead, amazingly, the householders invited them in, and they immediately noticed the tell-tale aroma of meth.

The officers immediately lost interest in the iPad, called for back-up, and a search began. Eventually, a staggering 780lb of the drug, in liquid and powdered form, was found, stuffed into duffel bags, boxes and thermos flasks.

It was one of the biggest-ever seizures of the notoriously evil substance – typically, San Jose turns up around 100lb per year.

'They probably thought if they didn't let us in, we'd suspect something,' said Assistant District Attorney David Tomkins. 'Or they thought, "I'll let them in – they probably won't find anything."'

At time of writing, the case was still pending.

*

TALKING OF APPLE, this burglar may not have been the dimmest crook ever, but he had the misfortune to be up against someone much brighter, Greg Martin.

Mr Martin, 29, is an IT security expert, and when his laptop was stolen during the London riots of August 2011 he remembered that he had installed an application called Prey, which meant he could track the £1,300 Apple MacBook once it was connected to the internet.

Macworld.co.uk takes up the story:

> Martin was having dinner in Luxembourg on a business trip when the first report came in.
>
> 'It was a really incredible feeling,' he said. 'I nearly fell out of my chair. I see this guy staring back at me, and I have his address.'

Martin watched for two hours as the 18-year-old thief cruised the net on the stolen computer, visiting Muslim religious sites (to pray for forgiveness, I suppose), shopping for a car on Autotrader and then trying to apply for a Tesco card in someone else's name.

Back to the Macworld account:

> It was only a matter of time before the young man logged into Facebook.
>
> In no time Martin had his name, where he graduated from school and his address. The man was just two blocks away, and Martin actually recognised a building that appeared in the background of a photograph taken by the webcam. He was even able to give police an estimate of what floor the suspect lives on.
>
> Officers, said Martin, had no problem finding their man.

*

JEROME SMITH IS not the only dumb criminal to decide that tattooing your face is a good idea, and he won't be the last.

However, he *is* probably the only one to tattoo himself with the word 'Genius' across his forehead… and to spell it 'Jenius'.

Smith, 27, already had an impressive rap sheet that included drugs offences, burglary and attempted murder when he decided to pistol-whip a pregnant woman in Cincinnati, Ohio.

To say the least, his tattoo is unusual, and it helped officers track him down swiftly. He was jailed for nine months.

*

DAVID WINKELMAN ISN'T   the brightest of sparks, which is why when a DJ offered 'a six figure sum' for anyone who would tattoo the radio station's logo on their foreheads, he went ahead and did it.

I urge you to Google Mr Winkelman – there's an excellent police mug shot showing him with a giant blue '93 ROCK' brand across his face.

Sadly for him, the DJ had – obviously – been joking, so there was no six figure sum forthcoming (and to make matters worse, the station soon changed its name to KQCS, Star 93.5, leaving Winkelman's head promoting something that no longer even exists).

He clearly ticks the stupid box, but why is he a criminal? Well, his appearance before a court for stealing a car, and subsequent spell in Iowa's Scott County Jail earns him the full title.

Eyewitnesses will find him hard to forget if he commits future crimes, too.

*

IN A WAY, NICHOLAS Webber is anything *but* stupid.

In fact, when it comes to computers, the young ex-public schoolboy is positively brilliant – which is how he came to head a worldwide cyber-crime empire by the time he was 18.

He was a wrong'un almost from the start – at school, he had used his talents to break into the computer system and delete details of his friends' detentions from their records.

But, after leaving, he moved up a notch or two. As the shadowy hacker behind 'GhostMarket', he stole the details of thousands of credit card holders and their accounts, and advised crims around the globe on how to create computer viruses and commit computer crime. He got away with at least £473,000, and could have stolen £15 million… but for what he did next.

Instead of lying low, he flaunted his wealth – posing for photos with wads of cash, or flashy cars (even though he hadn't passed his test), and wearing all the bling and designer schmutter that his greedy little heart could desire. Crucially, he also started living the high life in London's most exclusive hotels, and it was this particular piece of idiocy that proved his downfall.

When he tried to pay the bill at Piccadilly's Athenaeum Hotel – he was staying in the £1,600-a-night penthouse, with views of Green

Park and the London Eye – the receptionist became suspicious. Could this callow youth *really* have the means to settle these kinds of accounts? Was this his credit card... or was it stolen?

The cops were called, and the rest is history.

Scotland Yard – where detectives from the Met Police's Central e-Crime Unit had been after the Mr Big behind GhostMarket for quite some time – had finally got their man.

His laptop contained the details of 100,000 credit cards, and his room was full of business cards featuring Webber's online name 'N2C' and 'GhostMarket'.

Webber was arrested, bailed and then legged it to Majorca, where he booked himself straight back into the best hotels on the island, continued running GhostMarket and taunted the police with comments like, 'To be a Legend Carder u gotta be a ghost!' and 'F*** the Police!'

Eventually, he came home and was re-arrested and, in 2011, jailed for five years.

Luckily, he learned his lesson.

Not.

Webber made headlines again when he hacked into his prison's computer system from inside jail, after he was allowed to join an IT class...

*

OH, TOMMY. TOMMY, TOMMY, what were you thinking?

You're not, of course, the first prolific criminal to be locked up at Christmas. But you are probably the first to be jailed shortly after helping the police promote a scheme urging crooks to stay out of trouble – and out of jail – during the festive season.

Tommy Rouse, a 35-year-old from Bury, Lancs, was the face of campaign by Greater Manchester Police to have a crime-free (or at least a slightly less crime-fuelled) Christmas 2010.

Tommy was pictured holding up greeting cards with slogans such as 'Don't be a pudding' and 'Stay out of trouble'.

Having spent nine Christmases in jail for offences stretching over 21 years including burglary, car theft, assault and drugs, it looked like he might finally have turned his life around. He'd been given a chance by the police and probation services, who believed Tommy when he said that he wanted to spend the forthcoming Christmas with his five children.

'Think of your family and think of your victims,' he said, in an interview. 'It's not worth going in jail and losing your family and everything else. I've spent nine Christmases in prison. When you're in jail you're on your own routine, but it's when you get on the telephone to the girlfriend you think, "I should be home with the kids opening presents." You don't want to be locked up away from your family. This year will be different, the kids are already saying they can't wait for Christmas.'

Then he was caught taking drugs, which was a breach of his parole conditions, and it was back to jail.

'Tommy Rouse was given the chance to go straight and make something of his life,' said Superintendent Mark Granby. 'After 18 weeks on bail, he shattered the faith people had put in him by returning to drug use. This was despite the progress he had made in getting a flat, starting to take responsibility for his family, and being supported to take up a painting and decorating course. The message to people like Tommy is clear. You will be given a chance and support to turn your back on crime and become a useful member of society, but there are conditions. Fail to keep those conditions, and you will find yourself behind bars whether it's Christmas or not.'

*

THE FOLLOWING HEADLINE from *The Daily Record* says so much about the state of the criminal community these days:

DOPEY ROBBER rang police to get his getaway car back after they impounded it.

Along with an accomplice, Kenneth Johnstone held up a branch of B&Q in Bishopbriggs, near Glasgow, at knifepoint, and escaped with £750. A courageous and quick-witted witness followed the pair and took details of the Peugeot in which they drove-off. It was discovered by the police the next day at the home of Johnstone's mother, and was seized.

When Johnstone, a 35-year-old former soldier, found that his car had gone, he contacted the police to ask if they had any information about it – which led to him being identified from CCTV footage of the robbery.

The High Court in Glasgow heard in March 2010 that Johnstone had no recollection of the robbery, and that when he was arrested he broke down and claimed he wanted to 'turn the clock back'.

Judge Lord Bonomy jailed him for three years and nine months for a crime that he called 'ham-fisted'.

With all due respect to his lordship, the crime itself wasn't that ham-fisted – it was the stupidly failing to lie low after it.

*

BOBBY HODGKINS LIKED to steal motorbikes. He also liked to taunt the police by riding off on the stolen machines without a helmet – he knew that they wouldn't chase him if he wasn't wearing a helmet, because of all the criticism they would get if he fell off and hurt himself.

In August 2010, he was one of a gang which stole £20,000-worth of bikes from a showroom in Altrincham, Cheshire. Although the 24-year-old was later arrested, Greater Manchester Police came in for a lot of grief for that policy of not pursuing the men at the time.

Shortly afterwards, Hodgkins was bailed and pinched another motorcycle – a speedy Kawasaki off-road machine – during a burglary.

But that was the last one he ever stole, because he rode it into a Toyota van in Manchester a couple of days later and was killed.

He wasn't wearing a helmet at the time...

His family later paid tribute to him, saying, 'Bobby was a loving and loyal son who would do anything for his family. He will continually shine in our hearts forever.'

Maybe. He won't steal any more stuff, though.

*

DAVID EVANS WAS described in court as a 'clearly intelligent man', so perhaps the 57-year-old from Penarth, South Wales, shouldn't be featured here.

Yet his bizarre offence also included a series of blunders that were described as 'hopelessly wrong', and that's enough to qualify him for entry.

Evans, Bristol Crown Court heard in March 2012, had a 'grandiose sense of self-importance' which led to him deciding to impersonate a qualified barrister and represent a cannabis producer he'd met while in jail for offences of obtaining money by deception. Evans insisted that he was a 'senior advocate' at a London chambers, but it didn't take long for the judge in the case, Stephen Wildblood, to become suspicious.

It started with the way Evans had dressed – he was wearing a solicitor's gown but a barrister's wig. 'Although there may be circumstances in which a solicitor may wear a wig, it struck me immediately as strange,' said the judge. 'I was surprised to see the confusion of court attire.'

Then there was the matter of the submissions made by Evans which were, to use a legal expression, complete ballcocks.

'Wrong, completely wrong, in an elementary way,' the judge explained. Evans had argued that no confiscation hearing could take place after conviction, leading the judge to tell the court, 'This is simplistically wrong. It is the sort of thing you just look up in a book.'

Evans had also tried to suggest that the drug dealer's conviction was invalid because the cannabis plants had not been properly defined – this was also 'hopelessly wrong'.

When asked to cite his legal sources, Evans said that he was 'embarrassed' because he had left his legal books at home. He was even more embarrassed when a quick check with the Bar Council and Law Society revealed that he was neither a barrister nor a solicitor.

So Evans found himself back in court, this time in the dock, and being sentenced to 18 months.

Mrs Justice Laura Cox DBE told him, 'What you did was very serious and furthermore these offences are seriously aggravated by your previous conviction in 2005.'

On that occasion, he had impersonated a clinical psychiatrist.

*

WHEN COUNCIL WORKERS came across the five dumped bin bags, they assumed it was just another case of fly-tipping. But it wasn't normal household rubbish in the bags; it was a large collection of unusable off-cuts from cannabis plants, plus a few other items of more conventional rubbish – including, happily, a discarded letter with the name and address of the owner, one Anthony Smith.

The 41-year-old was arrested at his rented house at Shaldon, near Teignmouth in Devon, where officers found a cannabis factory containing 96 plants and capable, Exeter Crown Court later heard, of producing £32,000 worth of the drug in a crop.

Talking of drugs, the following headline in the *Shields Gazette* of 16 February, 2012, caught my eye: 'Man caught with drugs – on way to court to answer drugs charge'.

Kyle Smith was involved in a fracas at South Shields Metro station and when police turned up he denied any involvement, insisting that he didn't want to get into any trouble because he was on his way to Newcastle to be sentenced for possessing drugs. Then he dropped a wrap containing 22 diazepam tablets plus cannabis. Smith, a 22-year-old with an 18-month suspended burglary sentence hanging over him, was given a three month community order, plus a curfew.

*

IT'S NOT UNHEARD of for someone close to a gang to leak plans for a robbery, giving the police time to plan an ambush.

It *is* pretty much unheard of for the person doing the leaking to be the actual robber – *on his way to the job.*

'I'm coming to rob you,' said Albert Bailey (or words to that effect), in a call to a branch of the People's Bank in Fairfield, Connecticut. 'Get a bag of money ready – I'll be there in about 10 minutes. And I don't want any funny business – if you try anything there'll be a bloodbath!'

It ticks a few boxes – good organisational skills, planning ahead, making it quicker to get in and out, allowing the bank time to alert the cops…

Because that's obviously what happened, and Bailey, 27, was arrested by officers lying in wait at the bank.

'I've never had somebody call ahead and say, "Get the money, we're coming!"' Detective Lieutenant Michael Gagner told CNN. 'The guy is literally giving us a blow-by-blow, saying the robbery is going down. We were all kind of cracking up… definitely unusual technique.'

Bailey got nine years with no parole in 2011.

*

IT'S OBVIOUS TO all but the terminally stupid that dynamite is dangerous stuff, and not something that bungling amateurs should go anywhere near.

Unfortunately, the two thieves who struck in a bank in the Belgian town of Dinant late one night in September 2009 *were* bungling amateurs, and terminally stupid to boot.

In an effort to steal the cash inside an ATM machine, they placed a large amount of explosives around it.

When they detonated the explosives, they failed to open the cash machine – and even if they had, it contained internal security features designed to destroy the bank notes inside in the event of tampering. What they succeeded in doing was destroying the bank.

The explosion, at 3.20am, woke the entire town 65 miles south-east of Brussels. One of the robbers was found by police with serious head injuries, and died later in hospital. His mate was only discovered later that day, buried under the rubble. The men – one of whom was carrying Kosovan papers – were not identified.

'They were amateurs,' said bank spokesman Stephaan van der Baeten, perceptively.

*

A LITTLE NUGGET from Cork and *The Evening Echo* of January 2010:

> GARDAÍ are investigating the theft of an empty ATM in Cork city overnight. The raiders used a digger to steal the machine from a Texaco service station on the Model Farm Road at around 2.30am this morning. A van which was discovered a short distance away, is now being examined. The mini digger, used in the incident, had been stolen in Ballincollig last night.
> *Gardaí say the ATM had not been in use since December.*

*

THE FOLLOWING EITHER counts as bad luck or good luck, depending on your taste.

Russian robber Viktor Jasinski, 32, had hoped to fleece a hairdressing salon in Meshchovsk, presumably not expecting much resistance. But he was overpowered by the 28-year-old owner, a martial arts expert called Olga Zajac, who got him on the deck with a single kick and tied him to a radiator with the cable from a hairdryer.

Then she used him as a 'sex slave' for the next three days.

According to the account in *The Daily Mirror* in July 2011, he was force-fed nothing but Viagra, the whole idea being to 'teach him a lesson'.

Viktor went to the police after being released, and when officers arrested Olga she replied, 'What a bastard. Yes, we had sex a couple of times. But I bought him new jeans, gave him food and even gave him 1,000 roubles when he left.'

It sounds implausible, I know, and (assuming it actually happened) there is some doubt as to when it took place; it appeared in several UK papers in 2011, but is on *The Moscow Times* website, dated 15 April 2009. This, in turn, links to another website as its source, but this other site is no longer exists. All that said, sometimes stories do get picked up very belatedly from abroad – especially if they're as good as this one – and, while some of the details in the *Moscow Times* story are slightly different to those in the UK papers (for instance, Viktor was kept as a sex slave for two days, not three, and tied up with 'frilly pink fabric' rather than cable), the essentials are the same.

*

JARELL ARNOLD walked into a bank in Alaska, spoke to a cashier and then handed over a note saying, 'I have a gun. Give me all the money in your drawer.'

He then walked out with the equivalent of £400, thinking he had got away with it.

Unfortunately for him, he had forgotten the first rule of bank robbery: don't ask to check your balance first, and absolutely do *not* show the cashier your photo ID and give her your account number.

The *Anchorage Daily News* reported that the FBI arrested Arnold, 34, a few days later.

*

A VIOLENT THUG called Regan Reti and a car thief called Tiranara White were being led to prison after being sentenced when they saw their opportunity to escape.

The pair managed to wriggle free of security guards and make a run for it outside Hastings District Court on New Zealand's North Island in January 2009.

Their bold bid for freedom might have succeeded, too, had they not run either side of a lamp-post – forgetting that they were handcuffed together.

Moments later, the guards re-arrested the dazed pair as they lay in a heap.

CCTV footage of the incident, billed as 'one of the worst escape attempts ever seen', was later played for chortling viewers of the TV news in New Zealand, reported the *Daily Telegraph*.

Sergeant Dave Greig said, 'As they were being led from the Hastings police cells, they made a bolt for freedom. They fell over and were sprayed with pepper spray. But they got up and ran out of the court onto the street, across the road to a car park. That's where they met the pole – it was all over, rover.'

Reti, 20, and White, 21, were hauled back before the court to face fresh charges of escaping from custody.

*

DRUG DEALER ANDREW Law was spotted by cops and chased.

As he was legging it through Gloucester, he threw his jacket – containing £1,400-worth of cocaine and heroin and his mobile phone – into a residential garden.

The 23-year-old shook off the police, and the following day his mind turned to retrieving his drugs and phone.

So he texted the mobile saying, 'Who's got my jacket? I want the stuff back.'

Four minutes later, he texted, 'If you have got this phone, ring me!'

Then, 'I want my stuff!'

And then, 'Listen, we want the stuff from that jacket!'

Of course, Law thought that the jacket and its contents was in the possession of the person into whose garden he had lobbed it.

Sadly for him, it had been retrieved by the police, who were now reading the texts with increasing interest.

That interest was further piqued as his messages grew ever more frantic and threatening.

In short order, he sent the following:

> 'Listen, I want those f***ing drugs. I know which f***ing garden it was in so f***ing answer the phone!'

> 'I will burn your house down. Do you know who I am? Just answer the phone and we will do the deal!'

> 'Why won't you answer the phone? The chances are you don't know what you've got. You can make some money if you get in touch. Otherwise you'll get f*** all apart from a gun in your mouth!'

Before long, the text maniac was in police custody, being questioned about those messages and others which indicated he was a fairly serious drug dealer.

Derek Ryder, for the prosecution, told Gloucester Crown Court, 'Little did he know that the police had got hold of the phone, and they saw the texts, made the link to who he was, and went and arrested him.'

Law's arrest did not deter him. When he was freed on bail he started dealing drugs again – right outside Gloucester police station, where he was nabbed by CCTV cameras.

He had only just been released from a 42-month sentence, and in February 2009 he was jailed for six years.

A police source said, 'As dealers go, this guy wasn't the sharpest tool in the box. He was just a tool.'

*

A 'SCRAP METAL DEALER' suffered a terrible death after being electrocuted with 11,000 volts as he tried to steal copper from a derelict mill in Morley, near Leeds.

John 'Bod' Roberts was horribly burned, but still managed to stagger out of the building, get into his van and drive to his girlfriend's house nearby.

In a police statement read out in court, the girlfriend – Nina Hurley – said, 'At about 5.10am, I heard Bod's van coming along the street. I heard this strange screaming noise. Bod unlocked the front door and screamed, "Help me!" He came into the front room, sat in the chair and appeared to hyperventilate. He was shaking and his teeth were chattering. He was panicking. His skin was splitting on his hands and lips. His t-shirt had been burnt off. His face was all burnt – the only white was his eyes and teeth. His eye brows and eyelashes were all burnt.'

Roberts, 39, died in the burns unit at Pinderfields General Hospital 10 days later.

His inquest heard that the voltage was so high that the tools he was using to get at the copper wires probably melted completely. His injuries were caused by contact with a switch box, the effect of which would have been similar to blow-torching his skin all over.

There were prominent safety notices from Yorkshire Electricity warning of the high voltage and danger of death, but Roberts had ignored these.

Assistant deputy coroner Melanie Williamson – recording a verdict of death by misadventure – said, 'I am in absolute amazement how Mr Roberts managed to leave the transformer room, climb over the wall and into the car and drive over to Nina Hurley's house.'

The inquest heard how Roberts had gone to the mill two nights earlier with another woman whom he'd been seeing. They broke off the padlocks and climbed over railed walls in a bid to steal scrap metal; then they heard a loud buzzing noise, and wisely left.

Unfortunately, Roberts lacked the brains to know when he'd had a narrow escape, and went back two days later...

*

WHEN WILLIAM BIANCHI crashed his Mercedes cabriolet into a tree while drunk, he did what any responsible citizen would surely do and fled the scene.

But it wasn't hard for police to track him down – the Cheshire businessman was painted black and dressed as a Roman gladiator, and was accompanied by Superman.

The 38-year-old was tracked to a hospital in Macclesfield, where he was being treated for numerous cuts and bruises, and had singed hair from the burning car.

Officers said his frazzled appearance reminded them of Wile E Coyote after another run-in with Road Runner.

Macclesfield magistrates heard that he was on his way back from his goddaughter's 21st birthday party in Alderley Edge at around 5.30am when he had collided with a tree. It could have been very nasty – he was trapped inside the burning vehicle – but a passing taxi driver dragged him clear.

Bianchi was driven away, but officers found him at casualty shortly afterwards. He was around one-and-half times over the drink-drive limit.

*

IF YOU'RE GOING to commit a fraud, you might as well think big… but there are limits.

Charles Fuller smashed all the sane limits when he went into a bank in Forth Worth, Texas, and tried to cash a bogus cheque – for $360 billion.

The Register – picking the story up from the US TV channel NBC5 – reported that the 21-year-old wanted the cash to start his own record label.

That's a lot of studio time.

The Chase Bank cashier looked at the cheque – which was made out to 'Fulla Comp and Entertainment' and was drawn on his girlfriend's mum's account – and called the mum.

The Register says this was 'to see if it was legit', though this must have seemed more than slightly unlikely.

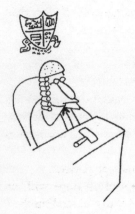

Fuller was arrested shortly afterwards, and the cops then found he was carrying a pistol and a small amount of cannabis.

Girlfriend Andrea Greer said, 'I wouldn't picture him doing something that stupid. I didn't think he'd do something this dumb.'

Her granny, Sharon Laird, said, 'I said, "Do what? Is he crazy?" We were just in awe.'

She added that if her family did have $360bn in the bank she would have been 'somewhere drinking margaritas', rather than chatting to reporters.

*

WHEN OMID CHIANG was caught by a speed camera doing 38mph in a 30mph zone, he pointed to the photo – which showed the green light flashing on the roof of his car – and asked the magistrates to let him off.

After all, he was a doctor heading to an emergency call…

The magistrates agreed, and he was allowed to leave with an absolute discharge, with his court costs paid through central funds.

If only the 26-year-old had left it at that, he'd have got away with a bit of a result.

Of course, he couldn't leave it at that.

Being stupid, he applied for a further £1,162.80 in costs to cover the employment of a locum doctor for the day he had spent in court.

The only problem with this was there was no locum, and there was no locum because Chiang wasn't a doctor.

Hampshire Safer Roads Partnership investigation team became suspicious because his application was full of spelling mistakes. They checked further and found that his name was not on the medical register. In fact, he was a medical sales representative.

He pleaded guilty to perverting the course of justice and deception at Southampton Crown Court, and in October 2007 he was jailed for 12 months.

*

MANY DRIVERS HAVE experienced the same sinking feeling as Chiang did – when a brown envelope drops on the mat with a speeding fine.

Not many have then gone on to fake their own deaths to avoid paying.

Shafkat Munir, 26, from Blackburn in Lancashire, knocked up a fake death certificate after cameras caught him three times and left him facing a bill of £180.

Then a man claiming he was 'Rashid Hussain' called the authorities, claimed Munir had died in Pakistan in 2002 and sent in the death certificate. It was written in Urdu, but was littered with mistakes.

John Davies, of Lancashire's Road Safety Partnership, said Munir's con was 'almost unbelievable'.

'His licence was clean before this spate of incidents, and he would have still been able to drive,' said Mr Davies. 'I have never known anyone go to such lengths.'

At Preston Crown Court, Munir admitted three counts of perverting the course of justice and was given three 12-month prison sentences, to run concurrently. He was banned from driving for 18 months.

*

IVAN SEGEDIN WASN'T much of a criminal – all he did was refuse to wear a seatbelt.

But he was caught and fined for doing so an astonishing 32 times – and he certainly fits the 'stupid' part of our description.

That's because, on deciding that he was fed up with being nicked, he considered two options.

One: wear the damned seatbelt.

Two: fashion a *fake* seatbelt device that he could install in his car to make it *look* like he was wearing his damned seatbelt, thus fooling the cops.

He chose the second, and knotted an extra belt on a long strap above the actual belt which then simply sat over his shoulder and created the illusion that he was driving legally.

No-one will know how long it would have fooled the cops for, sadly, because 39-year-old Ivan was killed shortly afterwards in a head-on car crash in New Zealand's North Island.

He suffered multiple injuries in the 'low-impact' accident – injuries from which the real seatbelt would certainly have saved him.

*

IF YOU BREAK into Chessington World Of Adventures with a plan to steal Spongebob the Bolivian squirrel monkey, you'd better come mob-handed – because he and his mates certainly are.

Marlon Brown, 23, found this out the hard way when he entered Spongebob's enclosure with nefarious intent, hoping to steal the £2,000 animal.

Brown thought it was going to be easy – after all, at their biggest squirrel monkeys are only a foot tall, and weigh just a couple of pounds.

But as he grabbed Spongebob, the nine other monkeys in the cage leapt on him and thoroughly kicked his backside.

Brown – part of an eight-man gang from Brixton which planned the raid on the Surrey zoo – did manage to get away with his prize, but he was forced to pay a serious price.

When police were called, they found Brown's blood, hair and skin scattered around the enclosure, and they were able to use this to catch their man via his DNA.

Meanwhile, Spongebob had been abandoned and was found safe and well in the streets of London a few days later.

Brown was jailed for a year.

*

JASON DENTON MUST have missed the cautionary tale of Marlon Brown – or maybe he just thought he was made of tougher stuff than the Brixton idiot.

Anyway, he broke into a house in Plymouth and got away with Addy – a three-year-old barn owl.

The plan was to sell her for a few hundred quid, and indeed it was all going well until he got back outside and found her large cage wouldn't fit into his little Ford Fiesta.

Oh, well, he must have thought, *I'll just take her out and carry her on my lap. What could possibly go wrong?*

What went wrong was Addy launched a ferocious attack on her captor as soon as he drove off. Within moments, he was desperately trying to fight off the scratching, pecking, screeching bird, as well as controlling the speeding vehicle.

This was only going to end in one way, and it did – the bleeding, yelping burglar managed to eject Addy from the car a few moments before he smashed into a wall at 65mph.

He was arrested shortly afterwards by police who had been called by householder Andy Godbeer.

Mr Godbeer, a shop porter, said Denton got 'exactly what he deserved'.

Addy suffered a dislocated leg in the ordeal, but was soon happily reunited with her owners.

Denton appeared, covered in bites and scratches, at Plymouth Magistrates Court, where he pleaded guilty to burglary and was given a suspended prison sentence and a curfew.

*

MIND YOU, BROWN and Denton got off very lightly, compared with the South African robber who ran away from security guards in Bloemfontein.

The BBC reported that the unnamed dumbass ran into the city's zoo and jumped into one of the enclosures to hide.

The tiger enclosure.

His body was spotted the next morning by keepers, police spokeswoman Elsa Gerber told the South African Broadcasting Corporation.

*

ALL INTERNATIONAL TRAVELLERS – at least those who are smuggling in an extra bottle of duty free booze – dread the question, 'Have you anything to declare?'

Very few can have made the confession uttered by a red-faced Robert Cusack.

A report into animal smuggling produced for the U.S. Department of Agriculture notes the case, and reads as follows:

> WHILE UNDERGOING a routine inspection at Los Angeles International Airport, a CBP (Customs and Border Protection) officer opened Cusack's suitcase. Imagine the surprise when a bird of paradise flew out. Careful examination found three more birds slipped inside nylon stockings and 50 orchids of an endangered species.
>
> 'When asked if there was anything else, he volunteered, "Yes, I've got monkeys in my pants."
>
> 'And indeed, Cusack had a pair of pygmy monkeys inside his pant legs. Cusack defended his actions by saying he was a concerned environmentalist who had purchased the animals in Jakarta, Indonesia and was taking them to a Costa Rican wildlife sanctuary. Nonetheless, he was arrested for smuggling.

He was sentenced to 57 days in jail after the incident in 2002.

*

YOU KNOW THAT scene from *The Godfather* when the film producer wakes up covered in blood with a horse's head stuck under his sheets?

Three wannabe mobsters in Tomaszow, Poland, tried something similar when local businessman Pawel Muszynski wouldn't pay their protection racket.

A police spokesman said, 'They decided a dead donkey would do the trick but they couldn't find one. So they grabbed a stork instead, which was easier to catch – they just shot it.'

The trio then left the stork's head with a warning note inside its beak on the bonnet of the shop owner's Ford Mondeo. It said: 'Pay up – or you'll end up like the stork.'

How did the cops track them down? It helped that they had *signed the note with their own, actual names.*

'It was a bit stupid of them really,' said the police spokesman. 'The dead stork was supposed to have been a warning – not a signpost to their front door. We will be charging them with unlawful killing of an animal, as well as extortion.'

At time of writing, the crooks faced five years in jail.

*

IT'S AN OFFENCE pretty much anywhere in the world to make prank calls to the emergency services, and rightly so.

Mohammad Baloch, also known as Mark Taylor, didn't appreciate this.

The New Zealander liked a drink, and when he'd had a drink he liked to call the North Shore police to declare his undying love for them, tell them what a great job they were doing, and pass on the latest jokes he'd picked up in the pub.

He did this, on and off, for a very long time, until he was caught by a wily operator who told him she'd only listen to his jokes if he gave her his address.

He obliged, and the following day he was up before the beak, where he was sentenced to 260 hours' community work and a fine of more than $700.

Judge Nevin Dawson told him, 'You've wasted an enormous amount of police time with your foolish actions.'

A police spokesman said, 'They generally weren't even very good jokes.'

*

THE AMBULANCE DISPATCHER in Coquitlam, British Columbia, had the following interaction with a certified dummy.

> Caller: 'Yeah, I'm having trouble breathing. I'm all out of breath. I think I'm going to pass out.'
> Dispatcher: 'Sir, where are you calling from?'
> Caller: 'I'm at a pay phone. North and Foster. Damn.'
> Dispatcher: 'Sir, an ambulance is on the way. Are you an asthmatic?'
> Caller: 'No.'
> Dispatcher: 'What were you doing before you started having trouble breathing?'
> Caller: 'Running from the police.'

A police car attended with the paramedics.

*

IN IRELAND, THE Gardaí mounted an investigation codenamed Operation Slope into the activities of an extremely dangerous gang.

The men were linked to a series of raids on cash machines across the country, including one in Tinahely, Co Wicklow, in May 2011, when six men used a digger to demolish a fair chunk of the front of a Bank of Ireland building.

One gang member shoved a gun in a man's face as he tried filming them tearing down the building. Twenty armed robberies over three years were linked to the men, along with two murders, and officers believed that in total the gang netted more than £400,000, and caused damage worth twice that.

The *Herald* newspaper recorded how Gardaí examined bank accounts held by gang members who were on welfare and unemployment benefits. Each month, between €30,000 and €50,000 was going through one particular account which belonged to a female member based in County Wexford who was also supposedly living off welfare payments.

There was only one obvious next step for the officers working on Operation Slope. Freeze that bank account. Which is exactly what they did, only for the criminal mastermind behind the gang – who was not named – not to notice, and to keep paying money into it for the next three months, thus basically handing it back to his victims.

'He went absolutely mental when he discovered the account had been frozen,' a source told the *Herald*. 'It just goes to show that he is not the smartest criminal in the world.'

*

STAYING IN THE Emerald Isle, meet the thieves who successfully stole not one but 10 top-of-the-range BMWs and their car transporter in April 2009.

Worth around £800,000, they were taken from Kinnegad, County Westmeath, on a Sunday evening, and driven to a building site in County Meath where the plan was to hide the lot behind a vacant house.

Ah. Unfortunately, the gang hadn't considered Mother Nature. It had been raining cats and dogs, and the site was a quagmire. As a result, the transporter got stuck in the mud, and sank up to its axles.

The thieves only managed to unload one of the cars before deciding to destroy the evidence by torching the others. The adjacent house was also gutted.

According to *The Sun*, a source said, 'It's hard to know whether these guys were amateurs or professionals.'

*

OF ALL THE STUPID ways to die, the method chosen by Wayne Mitchell takes some beating.

Mitchell, 20, was arrested along with his brother, Deangelo, 23, in December 2011 on suspicion of drug-dealing.

ABC News reports what happened next:

'A man died shortly after eating an ounce of cocaine hidden in his brother's buttocks in an attempt to avoid being caught with the drug.'

Police in North Charleston, South Carolina, released video footage of the pair sitting in the back of a patrol car, which appeared to show Deangelo persuading Wayne to swallow the drugs.

'You gonna eat it, you gonna chew it,' says Deangelo. 'One of us gotta do it. You the only one that don't have any strikes [convictions]. You my little brother... I'm gonna get life.'

Shortly afterwards, Dwayne struggled to breathe, bled from his mouth and died of cocaine poisoning.

Deangelo was sentenced to 15 years for drugs offences.

*

WHEN THE COPS called at Brian Mattert's house just after midnight in September 2010, he had been expecting them – he knew that allegations of domestic violence and assault had been made against him.

He wasn't planning to go down without a fight, but he knew they'd be carrying Taser stun-guns.

But Brian had had a brainwave.

What if he painted himself? They wouldn't be able to Taser him then, would they? It would be too dangerous!

When officers Joshua Thorton and James Womak arrived at the house in Cheyenne, Wyoming, with their Tasers drawn, Mattert – who had covered himself in white paint from head to toe – confronted them, saying, 'You see all this water-based paint? You shoot me with that, and you'll kill me.'

Well, it's a theory – but not one of which Einstein would have been proud.

They shot him, twice, but they didn't kill him.

They did arrest him, though, and – reported the *Wyoming Tribune*

Eagle – they charged him with a variety of offences, including resisting arrest and assaulting a police officer.

*

IT'S NOT ALL that unusual for daft people to impersonate police officers.

It *is* pretty unusual for them to do it in as stupid a way as the inappropriately-named Herman Justice.

The 56-year-old liked to pull over drivers and give them a talking-to, but he took it a bit far early one morning in 2010.

Indiana's *Courier-Journal* reported how Justice stopped a 41-year-old woman at about 3 am – using a flashing red police light – and ordered her out of her car at gunpoint.

He then asked his own girlfriend to call the *real* police 'for backup' – just like they do in the movies.

It obviously had not occurred to him that when they arrived – to find the poor, bewildered woman spread-eagled against her car with her hands up and this lunatic levelling his pistol at her – they might ask him for some ID.

They did, and quickly ascertained that he was not actually a policeman – in fact, he was an IT teacher.

He was quickly arrested, and found to be carrying a police baton and a holstered handgun and various badges (including those for a security guard and a defunct fire department from Florida).

More worryingly, state troopers also discovered five military-style guns, four knives and 446 rounds of ammunition in Justice's car.

And two dashboard-mounted video cameras... which had helpfully taped the whole thing.

*

IF YOU WERE planning to hire a hitman to kill your dad, how would you go about it?

Put the word around in the sleazy bars on the bad side of town, maybe?

Cosy up to a local gang leader?

Advertise the job on the Craigslist internet site?

If you answered yes to the last, you are as dumb as 23-year-old Megan Schmidt appears to be.

Because that's what police say she did, offering $10,000 to the successful applicant.

They responded to the advert, and sent along an undercover officer to meet Schmidt, from Dubuque, Iowa, to pose as the assassin.

Captain Bob Lynn, of Dubuque County Sheriff's Office, said they were surprised at how blatant she was. 'Usually this is something that takes place in a seedy bar or something like that,' he said. 'Who utilizes Craigslist? When you would respond to it, "Hey, I'm interested, what do you have?" she would immediately inform these people that she would like her father killed. She openly gives out the job specifics to anybody that responded.'

Several people tipped the cops off, and when the undercover officer showed up she allegedly gave him a photograph of her father and repeated that she wanted him dead.

'Basically, we came in and took her up on her offer,' added Capt Lynn said. 'We made sure she was serious.'

At time of writing, Schmidt was facing charges of attempted murder and solicitation to commit murder.

*

ACTUALLY, THE HIRING of hitmen is fraught with difficulty, for the stupid.

Jessica Booth was an 18-year-old aspiring model in Memphis, and she needed cash to pay for a new set of modelling photos.

She happened to visit some neighbours for a party, and in the kitchen she spotted a large block of Spanish/Mexican cheese called 'queso fresco'. It's white in colour, and resembles feta.

It also (apparently) resembles pure cocaine, and Booth put two and two together, reached five, and went looking for a hitman.

Her plan was to go to the house with the hired killer, slaughter all four people who lived there, and steal the 'coke'. She even went with him to a gun shop to buy a pistol.

Unfortunately, she knew about as much about professional assassins as she did about cocaine, or cheese for that matter, and the 'killer' she approached turned out to be a copper. In 2006 she was jailed for 15 years on four counts of attempted murder.

*

MICHAEL KUHNHAUSEN, WHO ran an 'adult bookstore' in Portland, Oregon, wanted rid of his estranged wife, Susan. Not wanting to get his own hands dirty, he hired a chap called Edward Haffey – who worked as a cleaner at the shop – for $50,000.

A few days later, Susan came home from her job as a nurse to find the bearded Haffey waiting for her in his kitchen with a claw hammer. He duly launched himself at Susan, hitting her in the head with the hammer... which was when things started to go awry.

'I could see in his eyes that he was here to kill me,' she told the Discovery Channel last year. 'He began to hit me in the head and face. And I knew, for whatever reason, he wanted to kill me, and I knew that I wanted to live.'

Haffey presumably thought his female victim would be a pushover; it was the biggest mistake he ever made. Susan grappled with him for some time – the whole ordeal lasted 14 minutes – and finally got the upper hand.

'I pushed him flat to the floor, and I got up on his backside and I leaned forward and I put my left arm under his neck, and I squeezed, and I said, "Tell me who sent you here, and I will call you an ambulance." I wanted him to be afraid and as terrified as I was.'

Stupidly, Halley tried to flip Susan off his back, and she tightened her grip – and in the process she strangled the hitman to death.

The police initially thought Halley was just a random intruder, but then they started asking questions. Like, how had he known her security code? And why did he have Michael Kuhnhausen's name and phone number written in the planner in the backpack he'd brought with him?

Kuhnhausen himself might be asking that question – and he was given 10 years inside in which to ponder it.

Susan, who did not intend to kill her attacker, said, 'I don't know that you ever get over having killed another human being. I've always said I don't take any pride in what I did. But I also feel no shame.'

*

WHAT WITH PETROL prices being so high these days, it's perhaps surprising more criminals don't try to steal it from other people's cars.

Those who are tempted are advised not to copy the methods employed by Herbert Ridge, of Mesa, Arizona.

Mesa police released CCTV footage showing the 37-year-old pulling up alongside a truck and using an electric siphon in an attempt to pinch some fuel.

To say he was not successful is an understatement.

As the *Phoenix New Times* drily reported, he set himself ablaze and 'based on the video-surveillance footage of Ridge going up in flames, it appears that he did not want to be on fire.'

In the footage, he immediately drops everything and hits the floor, rolling around in an attempt to put himself out. When that doesn't work, he hops back into his own pick-up and drives off, slightly erratically.

Police said he didn't get very far; after a few moments, the flames set his own vehicle on fire, so he bailed out of that, leaving it rolling into someone's garage door – setting that house ablaze, too.

Ridge then took off down the road, doing a passing impression of Usain Bolt, and actually made it to about two miles away before the cops caught up with him.

He was taken to the Maricopa County Burns Unit, and charges of theft, drink-driving, criminal damage, and possession of drugs were laid at his smoking door.

*

IF YOU EVER have the misfortune to be tagged, bear in mind that the whole point of the equipment is to track your movements.

This elementary fact escaped serial burglar Richard Almaraoui, who broke into a Norwich flat and was caught by a handy print-out which showed he had been there at the crucial moment.

The 33-year-old was jailed at the city's Crown Court for five years for that crime and five similar offences, plus the breach of a suspended jail sentence.

*

SOMETIMES, THE DUMBEST criminals earn our grudging respect for the sheer scale of their idiocy.

Michael Fuller might be one such.

The *New York Daily News* reported how the North Carolina man allegedly tried to use a fake banknote to buy some stuff at his local Walmart.

So far, so mundane.

Except that, police say, Fuller tried to pay with a million dollar bill (which the US authorities don't actually produce, for some reason).

Given that the items he was looking to buy came to $476, he would have got away with $999,524 in change.

If only those Walmart check-out girls weren't so switched on.

The 53-year-old was charged with fraud.

*

HOW DID THE police discover that 38-year-old unemployed security guard Sean Murphy from Doncaster owned an illegal firearm?

Because he had an irritating wart on the middle finger of his left hand and decided to use the 12-bore Beretta to remove it.

First, he self-medicated with several pints. Then, sitting outside his caravan, he took aim and fired at the blemish.

On the positive side, the operation was entirely successful, in that the blast removed the wart.

On the negative side, it also removed his finger.

And, still on the negative, Murphy was arrested and subsequently given a suspended sentence for illegal possession of a firearm.

The shotgun, it turned out, had been stolen in a 2009 burglary. Murphy told police he had found it under a hedge near his workplace in early 2011. His lawyer told Doncaster magistrates that his client 'has been a victim of his own stupidity when domestic pressures got to him'.

A rueful Murphy said, 'The wart was gone and so was most of my finger. There was nothing left of it, so no chance of re-attaching it.'

He got a 16-week suspended prison sentence, plus 100 hours' unpaid work. I suppose he should count himself lucky that the wart wasn't on the end of his nose.

*

IT WAS A NICE, soft target – a quiet branch of Burger King, with a day's takings on offer, and only two staff members on duty.

Or so thought 23-year-old Jeremy Lovitt and 19-year-old Gabriel Gonzales, when they allegedly made their move at Stockton, in California.

Police say they ran in with guns drawn, and ordered the employees to empty the safe – which they immediately started doing.

But the dumb robbers had made two crucial mistakes.

The first was that there were actually three employees in the restaurant.

The second was that the two men had left the engine of their getaway car running.

While they were standing over the safe, the third staff member snuck out of the back and drove off in the raiders' vehicle.

So when the hambunglers ran back out of the Burger King a

few minutes later, their ride was gone and they had no option but to employ Shanks's Pony.

As CBS Sacramento reported, the two men were arrested in a nearby field a few minutes later.

Joe Silva, from Stockton Police Department, said, 'The quick action from this employee allowed our officers to get on scene and arrest the suspects.'

The two men were facing robbery charges and many years in prison if convicted.

*

AUSSIE BURGLAR ANDREW Bawden was labelled his country's dumbest crook after leaving his own police charge sheet – detailing 24 offences – at the scene of one break-in and a DVD of his police interview at another the same night.

The 36-year-old from Bendigo went on his spree inside an hour of being charged and bailed over other burglaries.

'You get crooks sometimes who leave one thing that's stupid, but two things is extraordinary,' said Sgt Brendon Murphy. 'From the police perspective it's quite good. We appreciate people who leave this evidence for us. We're just thankful this numbskull's been nipped in the bud.'

Bawden – who was not long out of jail – pleaded guilty to around 30 crimes.

*

IF YOU'VE GOT it, *don't* flaunt it – at least, not if you got it by illicit means.

That might seem obvious enough, but there are plenty of stupid crooks – such as Kirsty Lane – who think it's a good idea to show off their ill-gotten gains.

Under the headline, 'Here Cons The Bride', *The Sun* told the story of how 29-year-old Lane fleeced her boss Peter Sutton of around

£200,000 – but was caught after inviting him to her ridiculously lavish wedding.

Mr Sutton was left speechless – and suspicious – by the extravagant bash put on by Lane, who was only a part-time accounts clerk.

There was a white Rolls-Royce, food by a celebrity chef and a fabulous firework display.

And a harpist, a saxophonist, and two bands.

And a DJ, and a magician, and a free bar for all the guests to enjoy.

Not to mention that the whole do was held in a beautiful – and very expensive – Tudor-built hall, and was to be followed by a honeymoon in Mexico.

Given that Lane earned less than £20,000 a year, Mr Sutton raised his eyebrows. Another director of the audio-visual company in Leyland, Lancs, joked with her that he'd have to check the accounts – at which she burst out laughing.

But a few days later, the firm *did* examine the accounts – and found them riddled with discrepancies, bogus invoices and dodgy payments. Company money had paid for *everything*, including the bridesmaids' dresses, and their thank-you gifts (tasteful jewel-encrusted iPods).

Lane, a mother-of-one, was arrested before she got chance to fly off on her dodgy honeymoon – which she didn't laugh about.

Jailing her for 20 months at Preston Crown Court in June 2012 – she admitted 10 counts of fraud and asked for another 112 to be taken in consideration – Judge Pamela Badley said Lane's behaviour was 'fraudulent from the outset', adding, 'This was a cynical exploitation of the small company for which you worked.'

Like many of the crimes contained here, the only thing funny about it is the culprit's stupidity. The consequences for those involved were anything but. Two people lost their jobs as a result of Lane's thievery. Mr Sutton told the local *Chorley Guardian*, 'It was like she was rubbing our faces in it. It was the wedding that first started to raise alarm bells. Up to that point we had no idea. She was always claiming poverty and didn't do anything that would tip us off. Then the wedding was the most lavish thing I've ever seen. I trusted her implicitly and this was how she repaid us. It was a very clever, incredibly devious operation that was calculated to the Nth degree. You read about these things, but you never think it will happen to you. It caused a lot of sleepless nights. We are not a large company, a lot of livelihoods depend on us. How it didn't sink us, I don't know. It's only through the sheer determination of the rest of the team that we are still here.'

Days after the wedding, while Lane was enjoying a mini-break in the Lake District, a routine problem with an account prompted Mr Sutton to investigate further. He found Lane had been using real invoices to suppliers to fabricate extra payments into her own bank account for more than two years. Such was the extent of her deception that it took two months to get to the bottom of it all.

For a final insight into the soul of this treacherous fraudster there's this: at one point, Lane wangled a £7,000 loan from the employers that she was systematically fleecing, claiming that she was struggling financially.

*

COCAINE DEALER GEORGE Kelly didn't particularly flaunt his ill-gotten gains, but his wife Julie Coyne did.

Neighbours grew suspicious that the pair were living beyond their means (they were on benefits) when 39-year-old Julie appeared one day with eye-popping new boobs.

When police raided their house, they found coke worth £30,000, Rolex watches and boxing memorabilia, including replica championship belts.

At Newcastle Crown Court, Kelly, also 39, was given two-and-a-half years inside for conspiracy to supply cocaine, while Coyne got a six-month community order.

'I think all of them should have been locked up for much longer than they got,' an unnamed neighbour told *The Daily Mail*, saving most of her anger not for drug-dealing Kelly, but the artificially inflated Coyne. 'If she's used ill-gotten gains to pay for plastic surgery then it's disgusting, it shouldn't be allowed.'

Another neighbour said, 'If she was going to spend all that money I can't believe she didn't get a facelift.'

And the *Mail*'s headline? 'Now that's a REAL drugs bust.'

*

BENEFITS CHEAT HAZEL Cunningham was just as devious. She claimed thousands for being a single mum when she was living with new husband Paul. She spent the money on holidays in Turkey and Kenya – not to mention a wedding in the Caribbean. The photographs of the ceremony in Barbados were so delightful that 47-year-old Cunningham posted them on her Facebook page. In February 2011, the mum of two from Ashford, Kent, was jailed for 120 days after admitting benefit fraud, and ordered to repay almost £15,000 that she had falsely claimed in income support, housing benefit and council tax benefit. She's got form for this, having been convicted in 2009 for claiming around £21,000 in incapacity, housing and council tax benefit while failing to declare that she was in work.

An Ashford Council spokeswoman said, 'Our investigators use Facebook as a routine tool when looking at someone's claim that they are single and not married.'

If you think that it's not clever for the council to divulge its investigative techniques, don't worry: the likes of Hazel Cunningham are unlikely to be caught reading this or any other book.

Among the comments on this story on the *Daily Mail* website was, 'I cannot believe these people are so stupid as to reveal their true circumstances on Facebook, while trying to pull off a benefit fraud! Only confirms my theory that the majority of Facebook users are as thick as Tesco Economy mince.'

*

FACEBOOK ALSO PROVED the downfall of Kim Stokes from Telford in Shropshire. Dim Kim claimed benefits on the basis that she was an unemployed lone parent who was separated from her husband, but wrote on her Facebook page, 'I've been with my hubby for 16 years and we're still very much in love.'

Meanwhile, husband Richard posted on *his* page, 'I am a loving, caring dad, I live in Telford and I am married to my soul mate, Kim.'

There were also pictures of the birthday cake made for her by her husband, holiday photographs and wedding anniversary messages. It was, as you'd expect, enough to land her in court – but not before she'd defrauded her way to £15,000 of taxpayers' money. In August 2010, Stokes, then 36, was given a 12-month community order and 200 hours of unpaid work.

Pamela Hughes, a 55-year-old from Pontypridd, south Wales, is another benefits swindler who claimed to be a single mum, and netted £35,000 courtesy of the taxpayer. Her fraud came to light when she was interviewed and investigators noticed her bracelet with the inscription '*Always yours, Brian*', and a date. It turned out that her lover Brian Wilcox had moved in a decade earlier.

She got six months jail, suspended for a year, and 200 hours' unpaid work.

'A scandalous and disreputable slur upon the good name of the law!'
The Honourable
Mr Justice Boniface

TOBY POTTS

For more from Monday Books, please see www.mondaybooks.com

SICK
NOTES
True Stories From The
Front Lines Of Medicine
DR TONY COPPERFIELD

'WONDERFUL'
Dr Phil Hammond

For more from Monday Books, please see www.mondaybooks.com

For more from Monday Books, please see www.mondaybooks.com

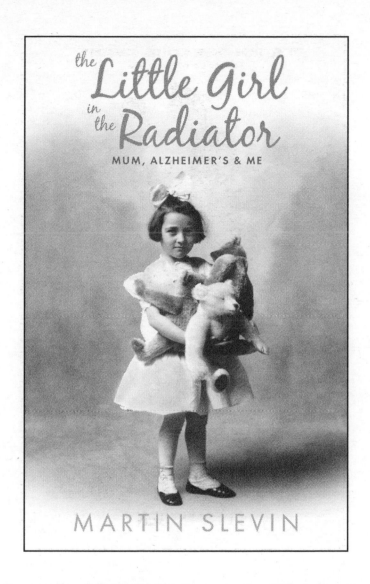

For more from Monday Books, please see www.mondaybooks.com

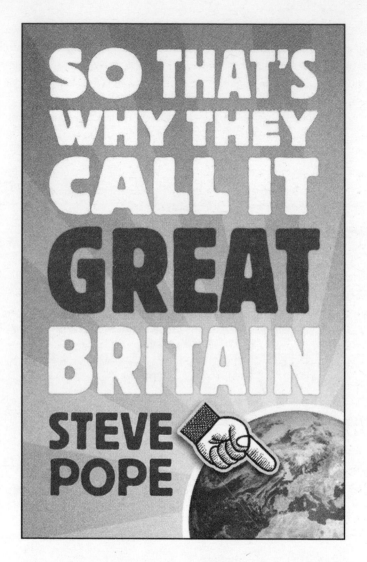

SO THAT'S WHY THEY CALL IT GREAT BRITAIN

STEVE POPE

For more from Monday Books, please see www.mondaybooks.com